John Henry Ellis

The Registers of Stourton, County Wilts, from 1570 to 1800

John Henry Ellis

The Registers of Stourton, County Wilts, from 1570 to 1800

ISBN/EAN: 9783337190590

Printed in Europe, USA, Canada, Australia, Japan

Cover: Foto ©ninafisch / pixelio.de

More available books at **www.hansebooks.com**

THE

Publications

OF

The Harleian Society.

ESTABLISHED A.D. MDCCCLXIX.

VIRGUS ... ... EG TIDE

THE GLORY OF CHILDREN ARE THEIR FATHERS

Registers.—Volume XIII.

FOR THE YEAR MD.CCC.LXXXVII.

THE

Registers of Stourton,

County Wilts,

FROM 1570 TO 1800.

EDITED BY

THE REV. JOHN HENRY ELLIS, M.A.,

Rector.

LONDON:

MITCHELL AND HUGHES, 140 WARDOUR STREET, W.

1887.

Introduction.

THE parish of Stourton is situated at the extreme west corner of the county of Wilts. It comprises the manors of Stourton, Bonham, and Gasper *alias* Brook. The two latter are in the county of Somerset, but the three together form one parish in the diocese of Sarum, in the poor-law union of Mere. The area is now stated at 3385 acres, but in 1851 it was 3543 acres. The population, according to the Census of 1801, was 649; it had risen in 1861 to 660; but at the last Census in 1881 it had fallen to 556.

The river Stour has its source in the six springs within the parish, which are represented on the coat of arms borne by the Stourton family.

This ancient family undoubtedly resided here in very early times, but there are no records to shew that they were landholders in Wilts till the reign of Edward I., when a Nicholas Stourton was holding one knight's fee here under the Lovells of Castle Cary, co. Somerset.[*]

In the fourteenth century the manor was held under that of Castle Cary by the Fitz Payn family. Early in the fifteenth century the Stourtons must have become owners of the manor, for in 1427 John de Stourton was granted a licence to enclose a park of 1000 acres, in 1428 he presented to the Rectory, and in 1448 he was created Baron Stourton. The property, largely increased by marriages with the heiresses of Moigne and Chidiock, remained in possession of the Stourton family till about the year 1720, when Edward the twelfth Baron sold the manor of Stourton and other lands to Henry Hoare, Esq. Old Stourton House, a large and curious building retaining all the internal arrangements of old baronial days, was then pulled down and the present mansion of Stourhead was built.[†]

---

[*] Aubrey's 'Wiltshire Collections,' edited by Canon Jackson, p. 392.

[†] See Leland's description in 'Wilts Archæological Magazine,' vol. i., p. 194; and Aubrey's account and sketch in 'Wiltshire Collections,' p. 390.

The manor of Bonham, which consists of only about 350 acres, probably belonged, in the fourteenth century, to the family of Bonham, who certainly held lands in Wiltshire. Sir John de Bonham was Knight of the shire in 1323, Walter Bonham was Sheriff in 1477, and John Bonham held the same office in 1550.* When the manor passed into the possession of the Stourtons is not certain. Sir R. C. Hoare ('Modern Wilts,' vol. i., p. 89) refers to a deed, dated 1665, by which Walter Bonham of Great Wishford, Wilts, granted a lease of Bonham House and Manor to Peter Pitney; also to an endorsement of the same deed which states that this lease was surrendered by Valentine Pitney unto the Hon. Thomas Stourton, and a new lease granted. An entry on page 65 of these Registers shews that a Mr. Stourton was living at Bonham House in 1611.

In 1785 the manor was sold by Charles Philip, sixteenth Lord Stourton, to the second Mr. Henry Hoare of Stourhead. The ancient Roman Catholic Chapel attached to the house was, however, reserved, and still remains the property of the Stourton family.

The third manor of Gasper, or Brook, containing about 1240 acres, belonged in 1693 to Robert Combes, but was sold in 1719 to Sir Isaac Rebow of Essex, from whose descendants it was purchased in 1799 by Sir Richard Colt Hoare, Bart.

The parish church (dedicated to St. Peter) formerly contained many memorials of the Stourtons. Aubrey mentions many escutcheons in stone and glass, all of which, with one exception, are now gone. There is, however, a fine monument with recumbent figures of Edward the fifth Baron, who died in 1536, and his wife Agnes Fauntleroy. These figures are engraved in Hoare's 'Modern Wilts,' vol. i., page 45. There are also some inscriptions on black marble slabs covering the Stourton vault, and as Sir R. C. Hoare's transcripts in 'Modern Wilts' are not quite accurate, I print them again here.

1. Hic jacet sepultus d'nus Johannes Stourton Baro' de Stourton,

---

* Canon Jackson, in a memoir of the Stourton and Hartgill tragedy, published in the 'Wilts Archaeological Magazine,' vol. viii., prints some letters discovered among the Marquis of Bath's papers at Longleat, which seem to shew that this Sir John Bonham was living at Brook in the parish of Stourton in 1553.

qui diem extremum clausit anno d'ni 1587, et regni Elizabethæ Reginæ Angliæ anno 28.*

2. Item hic jacet sepultus d'nus Edwardus Stourton Baro' de Stourton, frater prædicti Johannis, qui obiit septimo die Maii, anno Caroli Primi Regis Angliæ nono, annoque Domini 1633.

3. Item hic jacet sepultus dominus Gulielmus Stourton Baro' de Stourton, filius prædicti Edwardi, miles balnei, qui obiit vigesimo quinto Aprilis, anno Caroli Secundi Regis Angliæ vigesimo quarto, annoque Domini Dei 1672.

4. Item hic jacet sepultus dominus Gulielmus Stourton Baro' de Stourton, filius honorandi Edwardi Stourton, filii natu maximi prædicti militis balnei, primusque exclusorum† suæ domus Baronum in Parliamentariis apud magnates sessionibus et suffragiis, propter non ejurare fidem avorum sanctam, qui obiit septimo die Augusti anno Jacobi Secundi Regis Angliæ primo, annoque Domini Dei 1685.

All these four inscriptions are on one large slab.

5. Here lyes Francis Stourton, daughter of William Lord Stourton, obiit 4 Aug. 1646.

This inscription is on the same stone as No. 9, and *below* it.

6. Here lyes interred the body of Mary Lady Weld, wife of Sir John Weld, Knight, the eldest daughter of William Lord Stourton, who died the 15th day of May 1650.

7. Hic jacet Domina Margarita Stourton, filia Georgii Morgan, Arm., ex antiqua familia Lanthernham et Pentre; obiit die septimo Maii, Anno Dom. 1665. Carissimæ conjugi posuit Gulielmus Stourton, Ar'g'r.

The slab containing this inscription is now hidden by the floor of the seating, but both Aubrey and Hoare read it as above.

8. Here lyeth interred the body of the Honrble Thomas Stowrton, Esq., brother to the Right Honrble William Lord Stowrton, who died the 20th day of August anno d'ni 1669.

---

* The date of burial given in the Registers is Nov. 25, 1588. Burke's 'Peerage' gives the exact date of death, on what authority I know not, as Oct. 13, 1588. The 28th year of Elizabeth does not coincide with any part of the year 1587, but there is no doubt about the figures on the tombstone.

† Sir R. C. Hoare prints this "excelsorum;" and for suffragiis he gives "sheragiis."

This stone is now standing against the wall of the churchyard. There is no corresponding entry in the Registers.

9. Here lyes Winifred Lady Stourton, wife of William Lord Stourton, niece of Edward Duke of Norfolk, daughter of the Honourable Philip Howard, of Buckenham in the County of Norfolk, by Winifred his wife, daughter of Thomas Stonor, in the County of Oxford, Esq.; obiit 15 Julii Anno D'ni 1753, ætatis 26.

It may be well to state that Sir R. C. Hoare has not printed all the entries in these Registers which relate to the Stourton family. The list he gives in 'Modern Wilts,' vol. i., page 54, is far from complete.

The Registers here printed are contained in five books.

1. Old parchment book in fair condition, but wanting two leaves and badly stained in a few places. This contains:

> Baptisms, 1572 to 1687.   Marriages, 1578 to 1691.
> Burials, 1570 to 1599, 1610 to 1617, 1628 to 1685.

2. Parchment book in good condition, containing

> Baptisms 1691 to 1754.   Marriages 1702 to 1754.
> Burials 1691 to 1754.

3. Parchment book containing

> Baptisms 1754 to 1812.   Burials 1754 to 1812.

4. Parchment book containing

> Banns and Marriages 1754 to 1773.

5. Paper book containing

> Banns and Marriages 1773 to 1812.

The only years for which the Registers are missing are therefore as follows:

> Baptisms 1681 (part), 1687 to 1690   .   . Total 5 years.
> Marriages 1691 to 1701 .   .   .   .   . „   11 „
> Burials   1599 (part) to 1609, 1617 (part) to ·
>   1628 (part), 1681 (part), 1685 to 1690 . „   30 „

The transcripts relating to Stourton that are to be found in the Diocesan Registry at Salisbury begin in 1623, but there are many gaps in the series. They are referred to as "D. R.," and whatever they supply of the missing parts of the original I have printed in full in italic type. The Registers belonging to the Roman Catholic Chapel at Bonham do not begin before 1767, and till quite lately they have been very imperfectly kept. Permission has been kindly given me to examine them, and I have noted whatever additional information they afford. I have followed all the errors and variations of spelling that are in the original. The dates, however, have been uniformly printed; a capital letter has been used for the beginning of all names; and the words "was christened," "were married," "his wife," etc., have been omitted, the headings of the pages supplying the necessary information. The entries are printed in the exact order in which they occur in the original, but I have not thought it necessary to draw attention to this every time the chronological order is broken.

Many of these irregularities, and numerous cases of interlining, may be accounted for by the fact of a considerable part of the population being Roman Catholics, and therefore having their children baptized at Bonham Chapel. Evidently many of these Baptisms are recorded in the Parish Registers (see p. 21), and are sometimes interlined, and sometimes entered out of chronological order.

Many names are found in a variety of forms, some of which remind us strongly of the broad but pleasant sounds of the Wiltshire peasant's voice. For instance, Juhan, a form of the common Christian name Joan, has much more of the Wiltshire ring than a nearly similar form, Johan, which I have observed in the Registers of Mere. Perhaps I may be allowed to note here a curious way of describing illegitimate children which frequently occurs in the Mere Registers, thus: "Edward D., so named after his mother," or "bearing his mother's name."

There are still to be found in the parish, or in the immediate neighbourhood, a few of the names that are mentioned in the earliest parts of the Registers, viz. Davis, Ryall, Harding, Jupe, Smart, Parsons, Balch, Tabor, and Trimby.

J. H. ELLIS.

STOURTON RECTORY.
April 1887.

Rectors of Stourton.[*]

* This list is extracted from Institutiones Clericorum in com. Wiltoniæ, printed by Sir Thomas Phillipps at Middle Hill, 1825.

The Registers

OF THE

Parish of Stourton, Wilts.

A Register Booke of Christenings in the yeare of o^r Lord God 1572.

1572.

April 25	Richard Britten
April 29	Willm Lambe
May 25	Margerie Mychell
Aug. 17	Edward Lodwine
Oct. 19	Richard Warinor al's Pygat
Dec. 21	John Davis
Dec. 25	Richard Cowle
Feb. 2	Valentine Stylle
Mar. 22	John Spender

1573.

April 27	Judith Madox
May 4	Elizabeth Sandell
May 10	Margaret Kenison
Sep. 14	John Bashe
Oct. 25	Walter Marten
July 26	Willm Sandell
Dec. 20	Rynold Briten s. of Wm Briten
Nov. 29	Tomson Sutter d. of Tomas Sutter
Feb. 1	John Jeffreys al s Leuersedg
Feb. 8	Dorithe Davis d. of Robt Davis
Feb. 15	Valentine Lambe s. of Wm Lambe

1574.

Sep. 14	Eme Rioll d. of Leonard Rioll
Nov. 7	Katherine Kenisone
Nov. 28	Valentine Hardinge

1575.

Dec. 28	Thomas Simes
Oct. 22	Willm Briten
Oct. 30	John Sandell s. of Frannces Sandell
Jan. 18	Juhan Kenison

1576.

May 18	. . . .* Davie
July 11	John . . . .*
Aug. (?)	Marye d. of Robt Davie
Aug. 3	Richard S . . . .* elt
Sep. 5	John Bor . . . .*
Sep. 15	John Satter
Oct. . .	John Lambe s. of Wm Lambe
Nov. 1	Roger Genigs†
Nov. 28	. . . .* Sandell d. of John Sandell
Jan. 6	. . . .*
Jan. 11	. . . .* ner

1577.

Mar. 24	Marye Britten
April 26	. . . .* Stile
May 8	Will'm Lambe
May 17	Juhan Rioll
June 28	Margaret Bradden
Sep. 8	Thomas Davie
Jan. 26	John Satter
Mar. 8	Thomas Sandell

1578.

May 23	George Rioll
July 18	Will'm Rioll
Jan. 1	John Britten
Jan. 9	John Bradden
Jan. 9	Elizabeth Lodden
Nov. 25	Juhan Baker

1579.

April 3	Catherine Hardinge
May 26	Richard Sandell
May 31	Ralfe Martten

* Illegible. † For *Jennings*.

B

June 5	Christian Hill
June 14	Alice Stile
June 6	John Jooppe
June 16	Fraunces Jooppe
July 10	John Sandell
Oct. 9	Annes Lambe
Feb. 14	John Tomlen

1580.

April 29	John Tooppe
May 1	Katherine Davie
July 6	Tomsen Lambe
Sep. 7	Juhan Davie
Sep. 14	John Briten
Oct. 26	Juhan Bradden
Jan. 13	Richard Sandell
Jan. 22	John Parett
Jan. 29	James Bennett
Mar. 5	Juhan Flatcher
Mar. 10	Juhan Style

1581.

June 3	Elizabeth Jooppe
June 5	John Dean
July 7	Juhan Davie d. of Charles Davie
July 22	Mary Cooffe & Juhan Cooffe
Oct. 8	Anne Kirkin
Oct. 14	Walter Sandell
Oct. 15	Tomsen Lodden
Dec. 28	Tomsen Sandell
Jan. 7	Walter Hill
Jan. 14	George Suter

1582.

May 24	John Lambe
Aug. 5	Will'm Davis
Sep. 23	Juhan Bennett
Dec. 28	Henry Tayler
Dec. 31	Jane Billet
Jan. 7	Als Style
Feb. 20	Jane Tooppe
Mar. 8	Walter Britten

1583.

June 21	Edith Davie
July 14	Thomas Rioll
Oct. 3	Bartholomewe Bradden
Oct. 11	John Rogers
Oct. 12	Richard Cooffe
Oct. 15	William Caulpin
Nov. 11	John Dean
Jan. 5	Robert Sandell

1584.

April 5	Elizabeth Bennett
Jan. 7	Juhan Watts
April 24	Juhan Jooppe

May 6	Philippe Rioll
Feb. 27	John Stile
Aug. 14	Elizabeth Tobye
Sep. 3	Walter Lodden
Sep. 6	Edward Baylie
Sep. 13	Eme Hill
Nov. 1	Annes Tayler
Dec. 11	Tomsen Britten
Dec. 14	Thomas Tooppe
Mar. 7	Juhan Browne

1585.

July 3	Jane Byllet
July 3	Walter Parrett
Aug. 11	Elizabeth Sandell
Jan. 19	Elnor Spindleton
Feb. 11	Thomas Bennett
Feb. 24	Juhan Chamberlayne

1586.

April 1	Juhan Caulpin
April 8	Juhan Hill
May 22	John Cooff
May 28	Juhan Dean
June 1	Juhan Tooppe
June 12	Fraunces Rogers
Aug. 24	Will'm Baylie
Sep. 4	John Toby
Sep. 11	John Davie
Sep. 11	Leonard Sutter
Nov. 20	Thomas Britten

1587.

April 29	Annes Orpin
June 20	Marye Tayler
Aug. 30	Walter Sandell
Jan. 28	Annes Browne

1588.

April 8	Edith Davie
July 22	John Tooppe
Nov. 24	Juhan Hill
Jan. 1	Steven Dean
Feb. 1	Mary Toby
Feb. 9	Margarett Tayler

1589.

Feb. 22	Agnes Bradden
Sep. 22	Alsse Tayler

1590 & 1591 & 1592.

"I find none put in the other register booke but leaft out."

1593.

April 7	Margaret Veiven
June 2	Annes Chamberlene
July 22	Will'm Morgan

Aug.	17	Juhan Davis
Sep.	30	Willm Lawnder
Jan.	20	Walter Northest
Feb.	17	Willm Hardinge

1594.

April	15	Dorithe Maunsell
May	29	John Rosse
July	21	Thomas Rogers
Nov.	10	John Style
Dec.	1	Jane Pittney
Jan.	1	Als Barnes
Jan.	4	Edith Mericke
Jan.	12	Willm Sandell

1595.

April	6	Henry Edwards
April	18	Margarett Dean
Sep.	15	Fraunces Toby
Oct.	12	Jane Browne
Oct.	17	Rinold Juppe
Jan.	25	Mawd Elis & Elizabeth Elis
Feb.	1	Mary Davis

1596.

April	14	Dorithe Hardingo
April	18	Juhane Spender
May	20	Juhane Frey
May	22	Fraunces Mericke
May	26	Elizabeth Davis
Nov.	27	John Kenison
Jan.	30	Mary Rosse
Feb.	24	Juhan Britten

1597.

April	1	Willm Rogers
April	24	Valentine Pittney
June	20	Edward Blanfford
July	17	Roger Stile
Sep.	26	Catherine Davis
Oct.	7	Thomas Harding

1598.

April	2	John Sandell
May	30	Willm Meiricke
June	11	Margarett Edwards
June	20	Alexander Ingram
July	17	John Presseley
Aug.	24	Fraunces Elis
Nov.	5	Catherine Sandell
Jan.	6	John Sandell
Jan.	6	Anne Dean
Mar.	14	Constance Britten
Mar.	16	Jaune Shard
Mar.	18	Elizabeth Sandell

1599.

| April | 29 | Charles Davis |
| May | 1 | Edward Toby |

Aug.	5	Mary Hardinge
Jan.	12	Fraunces Stourton s. of the right honorable Lord Edward, lord of Stourton
Jan.	19	Elizabeth Meiricke
Mar.	2	Robert Kenison
Mar.	10	Susan Rose
Mar.	22	Marye Blanford
Mar.	29	Mary Greene

1600.

June	1	Robert Hollowaye
July	13	Margaret Davis
July	27	Jane Godffrey
Nov.	9	Walter Milborne
Nov.	9	Robt Juppe
Nov.	16	Juhan Ingram
Nov.	23	Jane Edwards
Feb.	1	Richard Britten
Mar.	3	Fraunces Sandle

1601.

April	25	John Keniston
May	9	Willm Gibson
July	6	Jane Prestely
Aug.	9	Valentyne Sandle
Aug.	17	Sellina Toboy d. of Willm Toboy
Jan.	10	Edyth Chicke the reputed d. of John Loddon
Jan.	24	Tomsonne Davis d. of Charles Davis
Jan.	29	Roberte Borrowe s. of John Borrowe

1602.

April	4	Elizabeth Sandel d. of John Sandel
May	23	John Blanford s. of William Blanford
June	2	George Stile s. of Valentine Stile
July	20	Margerie Gibbes d. of Richard Gibbes
July	27	Elizabeth Halloway d. of Thomas Halloway
Oct.	20	James Kennison s. of William Kennison
Dec.	5	Alexander Davis s. of Robt Davis
Dec.	25	Peter Pitney s. of Pitney
Jan.	5	Francis Hardin d. of Thomas Hardin
Feb.	24	Paul Harding s. of Roger Harding
Mar.	4	Martyn Hardinge s. of James Hardinge
Mar.	12	Edward Borrough s. of John Borrough

1603.

July 6	Jone d. of Thomas Kinge
Oct. 26	Elizabeth Godffrae d. of Walter Godffrae
Nov. 9	Charles Spender s. of George Spender
Dec. 16	Samuell Willson s. of Andrew Willson
Dec. 21	Thomas Ryall s. of Robᵗ Ryall
Feb. 12	Robert Irons s. of Robert Irons & Jone
Mar. 18	Gillian Holloway d. of Thomas Holloway & Jone
Mar. 21	Anne Brittan d. of Richard Britton & Agnes

1604.

April 20	Thomas Sandall s. of Robert Sandall
Aug. 24	John Sandall s. of John Sandall & Winefrid
Sep. 15	Edith Milborne d. of Richard Milborne & Gillian
Sep. 24	Edward Gibbes s. of Richard Gybbes
Oct. 14	Richard Burrough s. of John Burrough
Dec. 3	Jane* Greene s.† of Alexander Greene
Jan. 20	John Aford s. of James Aford
Feb. 6	Elizabeth Blanford d. of William Blanford
Feb. 12	Agnes Leaver d. of William Leaver
Feb. 13	William Dauy s. of Robert Dauy
Mar. 3	Jone Kennisson d. of Robert Kennisson

1605.

April 3	William Kennison s. of Willᵐ Kennison
July 22	Edward Stourtoⁿ s. of Lᵈ Edward Sᵗ
Oct. 3	Mary Sandell d. of Robert Sandell
Oct. 10	Joane Riall d. of Robert Ryall
Oct. 17	Tampson Pitny d. of Peeter Pitny
Dec. 10	John Saundell s. of John Saundell
Dec. 10	Gillian Hilgrove d. of Frauncis Hilgrove
Dec. 20	Frauncis Joope s. of John Joope

* *Elizabeth* written first and struck out.
† So in original.

1606.

July 13	Roger Rendole s. of Joseph Rendole
Dec. 7	William Greene s. of Alexander Greene
Feb. 8	John Russell s. of John Russell, Clerke
Feb. 14	Rachell Day d. of Robᵗ Day

1607.

April 4	Alice Fulford d. of Robert Fulford
April 22	Joane Saundell d. of John Saundell
(?) 17	Ellyn Davis d. of . . . .*
Dec. 21	Susan Saundell d. of Robert Saundell
Jan. 4	John Davis & Robert Davis sons of Alexsaunder Davis
[blank]	John King s. of John King†
Dec. 9	Walter Barnes s. of Robert Barnes
Jan. 12	Tampson Riall d. of Robert Riall
Jan. 31	Annis Avord d. of James Avord
Feb. 24	John Cayford s. of Thomas Cayford

1608.

Mar. 29	John Riall s. of John Riall
Mar. 30	Nicolas Bowne s. of Thomas Bowne
April 18	George Davis s. of William Davis
May 28	Willᵐ Joup s. of John Joup
Nov. 28	Joane Saundell d. of John Saundell
Dec. 7	Toby Daye s. of Robert Daye
Dec. 9	William Godfry s. of Walter Godfry
Feb. 12	Mary Barnes d. of Robert Barnes
Feb. 12	Robert Blanford s. of William Blanford
Mar. 7	Ann Greene d. of Alexsaunder Greene
Mar. 9	Thomas Ashford s. of Thomas Ashford
Mar. 16	John Riall s. of John Riall
Mar. (?)	Henry Gibbes s. of R . . . .‡ Gibes

1609.

April 3	Roger Stile s. of Roger Stile
Nov. 7	Anne Davis d. of Robert Davis

* Ink faded.   † Interlined by another hand.
‡ Probably *Richard*. See 1604.

Dec.	9	Robert Parsons s. of Willm P'sons
Feb.	6	Darrothy Erbery d. of Thomas Erbery
Mar.	4	Mary Saundell d. of John Saundell

1610.

Mar.	26	Robert Saundell s. of Robert Saundell
Mar.	30	Thomas Davis s. of Alexsaunder Davis
June	21	William Kinge s. of John Kinge
July	8	Thomas Saundell s. of John Saundell
July	11	William Bacon s. of Frauncis Bacon
July	29	John Dean s. of John Dean
Aug.	3	Peeter Saundel s. of Robert Saundell
Oct.	6	Hughe Burrowes s. of John Burrowes
Oct.	6	[blank] Flewellen the [blank] of Geoffery Fluellen
Nov.	4	Joan Sandall d. of Thomas Sandall
Nov.	5	Edith Daye d. of Robert Daye
Jan.	20	Edith Cayford d. of Thomas Cayford
Feb.	6	Emeline Ryall d. of Thomas Ryall
Mar.	17	John Kenison s. of Willm Kenison

1611.

April	9	Alexander s. of Alexander Greene
May	19	Robert s. of Robert Ryall
July	6	Mary d. of Walter Tabor
July	7	Elizabeth d. of Mr Robert Barons
Sep.	8	James s. of James Auford
Oct.	27	Joane d. of John Parrett
Oct.	28	Joan d. of John Ryall
Dec.	8	Joan d. of John Lodwin
Jan.	5	Jane d. of Mr Robert Fulford
Feb.	7	Ann d. of Charles Midwinter
Feb.	13	Richard s. of Benjamin Strong
Mar.	15	Christian d. of William Britaine

1612.

Mar.	25	Mary d. of Jupe
May	18	Rachel d. of John King, P'son
July	12	Elizabeth d. of Francis Bacon
Aug.	12	Joan d. of John Edwards
Dec.	26	Robert s. of John Lodwin
Feb.	5	Jane d. of Thomas Sandall
Feb.	10	Isaac s. of Willm Cuffe
Feb.	10	Dorothy d. of John Sandall

1613.

April	9	Robert s. of Robert Daye
April	9	Alice d. of Alexander Davis
May	30	Gualter s. of John Sandall
July	2	Francis s. of Francis Sandall
July	28	Joan d. of Robert Barnes
Sep.	12	Mary d. of John Parret
Jan.	29	Anne d. of John Dewe
Jan.	30	Henry s. of Willm Henckstrige
Feb.	5	Joan d. of John Ryall
Mar.	6	Elizabeth d. of Jo. Bartlet

1614.

June	19	Margery d. of Francis Bacon
June	26	John s. of Alexander Green
June	26	Mary d. of Willm Brittain
Aug.	14	John s. of John Cuffe
Sep.	13	John s. of Walter Lodwin
Dec.	16	Steven s. of John Bradden
Dec.	18	Willm s. of Robert Sandall
Feb.	11	Robert s. of Willm Toop
Feb.	12	Joan & Edith das. of Walter Tabor

1615.

April	16	Rob. s. of Thomas Ryall
May	12	Mary d. of Jo. Parret
May	18	Rob. s. of Rob. Barnes
May	29	Mary d. of Jo. Dewe
June	16	Richard s. of Jo. Deane
June	16	Mary d. of Cutbert Tremby
July	23	William s. of Rob. Brittin
Aug.	30	Henry s. of William Henstridge
Sep.	19	Joane the supos^d d. of Rob. Jians
Dec.	15	Robert s. of Thomas Sandall
Dec.	29	John & Walter & Susan children of John Lodwin

1616.

May	5	John s. of Alexander Greene
May	12	John s. of John Cuffe
June	30	Steven s. of Steven Bell
July	16	Richard s. of John King
July	17	Mary d. of Robt Barnes
Nov.	1	Susan d. of William Brittin
Dec.	8	Frauncis s. of Francis Sandall
Dec.	14	Alexander & Joane children of Alex. Davis
Jan.	19	Mary d. of Walter Taber
Jan.	26	William s. of Willm Ryall
Feb.	5	Tomason d. of Jo. Braden
Mar.	2	James s. of Cutbert Tremby

1617.

Mar.	25	Mary d. of Jo. Sandall
Aug.	26	. . . .* d. of John Parret

* Illegible.

Sep. 28	....* d. of Walter Lodwin
Sep. 29	........*
Oct. 12	....* Ryall
Nov. 9	....* Barnes
Dec. 3	........*
Dec. 4	........*
Mar. 1	Thomas s. of Robᵗ Day
Mar. 14	Maud d. of Lawrence Role
Mar. 16	Eliz. d. of John Lodwin

1618.

May 17	Jane d. of William Henke- stridge
May 20	Mary d. of James Alford
May 25	Mary d. of Thomas Ryall
June 17	Valentine s. of Jo. Bradden
July 9	Nicholas s. of John King
July 12	Eliz. d. of Thomas Ashford
Sep. 4	John s. of Eliz. Lodwin
Sep. 24	Mary d. of John Deane
Oct. 25	Morrice s. of Barbara Duffin
Nov. 22	Rob. s. of Alexander Greene
Nov. 30	Anne d. of Anne Havsam
Dec. 11	Marg. d. of Jo. Bartlett
Feb. 14	Susan d. of Walter Tabor
Feb. 27	William s. of Leonard Shuter

1619.

May 13	Edith d. of William Brittin
May 16	Richard s. of John Cuffe
June 2	Elizabeth d. of Thomas Sandall
Nov. 19	Anne d. of John Lambe
Dec. 29	Richard s. of Richard Bayly
Mar. 5	Walter s. of Thomas Tabor
Mar. 12	Thomas s. of Francis Sandall
Mar. 12	John s. of Cutburt Tremby

1620.

April 15	An d. of Laurence Roule
May 10	John s. of John Perce
May 20	Mary d. of Anne Browne
July 10	Grace d. of Robert Barnes
Oct. 1	John s. of John Bradden
Dec. 27	William s. of Thomas Riall
Feb. 7	Francis d. of John Deane
Feb. 12	Christian d. of John Stile, tanner
Feb. 14	Maude d. of John Stile
Mar. 21	Elizabeth d. of John Edwards

1621.

Aug. 4	John Sandall s. of John Sandall
Aug. 24	Matthew s. of Leonard Shuter
Sep. 4	John s. of John Davie
Sep. 26	Cicel d. of Willᵐ Hentstridge
Nov. 4	George s. of Alexander Green
Nov. 11	John s. of John Lamb

* Illegible.

Dec. 6	Marie d. of John Bartlett
Dec. 11	Walter s. of Walter Tabor
Dec. 20	Marie d. of Thomas Sandall
Jan. 14	Margery d. of Edward Wind- sore
Jan. 20	Francis s. of John Cuffe
Jan. 30	Valentine s. of John Sandall

1622.

April 5	Anne d. of John Sandall
April 20	Alexander s. of John Deawe
May 3	Margaret d. of Walter Lodding
June 10	William s. of Henrie Edwards
July 14	William & John sons of Wil- liam Britaine
Oct. 6	William s. of Nicholas Dyar
Nov. 14	Leonard s. of William Ryall
Jan. 8	John Hewlett s. of Roger Hewlett, Curat
Jan. 15	William s. of Laurence Rolle
Mar. 2	John Stile s. of John Stile

1623.

April 5	Marie Perrie d. of John Perrie
April 15	Robert s. of John Kinge, Docᵗʳ of Divinitie
May 18	Nicholas s. of Edward Windsore
Sep. 12	John s. of Thomas Reede
Dec. 4	Charles s. of John Davis
Dec. 7	William s. of John Sandl., iun.
Feb. 15	Matthew s. of Francis Sandl.
Feb. 19	William s. of Henr. Barnes*
Feb. 27	Thomas s. of William Stile
Mar. 2	Richard s. of Richard Smith
Mar. 17	Walter s. of Walter Tabor

1624.

Mar. 31	Marie d. of William Hinck- stridge
April 25	Andrew s. of Cutbert Trimbey
April 27	Joh. s. of Henrie Edwards
June 6	Andre. s. of Joh. La'b
Sep. 26	Marie d. of Joh. Edwa:[rds]
Oct. 27	Alixet d. of Thom. Ryole
Nov. 11	Elizab. d. of Alexa'd. Gree:[ne]
Nov. 25	Avice d. of Joh. Perrie
Dec. 2	John s. of Thoma. Sandle
Dec. 5	Agnice‡ d. of Joh. Foreward
Dec. 5	Joh. s. of Joh. White
Feb. 3	Adam s. of Joh. Cuffe
Feb. 27	Henrie s. of Roger Hew: [lett], Ministʳ§
Mar. 10	Thomas s. of William Brita:[ine]
Mar. 10	Mari. d. of Rich. Smith

* In D. R. Barens. † In D. R. Aulce.
‡ In D. R. Aunice. § In D. R. Hulet.

1625.

Aug. 24	Edmond & Elizabeth children of John Swetna'	
Sep. 8	Elizabeth d. of Doct' Kinge	
Sep. 16	Margaret d. of Leonard Sutor	
Oct. 10	Nicholas s. of John Sandle*	
Oct. 16	William s. of John Stile†	
Nov. . .	Charles s. of William Holdway	
Feb. 24	Francis d. of John Sandle the yo'ger‡	
Mar. 5	Laurence s. of Laurence Roles	
Mar. 12	Henrie s. of Henrie Edwards	

1626.

Mar. 26	Thomas s. of Edward Winsore
Mar. 30	Valentine s. of William Ryole
April 3	Edward s. of Thomas Reede
April 30	Nicholas s. of Robert Barnes
May 7	Edward s. of William Henckstridge
July 23	Tomson d. of Walter Taber
Aug. 2	Roger s. of Thomas Sandle
Nov. 3	William s. of John Lambe
Dec. 10	Margaret d. of John Davis
Jan. 10	Charles s. of Francis Ellice
Feb. 11	Elizabeth d. of Henrie Barnes
Feb. 23	Rachel d. of Roger Hewlett, Curat

1627.

May 6	Anne d. of Richard Smith
July 29	Margaret d. of John Forwood
Aug. 10	Catherine d. of Henrie Edwards
Sep. 12	Francis d. of William Britaine
Sep. 16	Richard s. of Walter Bord
Nov. 23	Joane d. of William Holdway
Nov. 25	Edith d. of Thomas Sandle

1628.

May 22	Marie d. of John Cuffe
May 25	Elizabeth d. of Thomas Ryol
June 4	Elenor d. of David White
Aug. 4	Anne & Francis das. of Cutbert Trimbey
Sep. (?)	Timothie s. of John Sandle
Sep. (?)	Mathew s. of Josias White
Dec. 1	Edbert s. of Edward Sewter
Feb. 1	Richard s. of Richard Smith
Feb. 5	Catherine d. of Valentine Pitney
Feb. 25	Marie d. of John Lambe
Mar. 8	Samuel s. of John Sandle
Mar. 22	John s. of Laurence Rolles

* In D. R. ye younger.
† In D. R. ye younger.
‡ In D. R. the yo'ger is omitted.

1629.

April 26	Edward s. of Henry Edwards
May 3	Philip s. of Walter Taber
May 17	William s. of Thomas Reede
June (?)	Joane & Elizabeth das. of William Henckstridge
July 29	John s. of John Swetnam
Aug. 24	Elizabeth d. of John Lodwin
Sep. 22	Thomas s. of Henry Barnes
Sep. 27	William s. of John Davis
Nov. 8	Joane d. of William Bernard
Nov. 29	Francis d. of William Holdway
Dec. 6	Robert s. of Robert Sheepeheard
Feb. 4	John s. of Richard Smith
Feb. 24	Mathew s. of William Britaine
Mar. 7	Margaret d. of Josias White

1630.

May 16	Roger s. of Roger Hewlett, Curat
May 16	John s. of John Edwards
May 23	John s. of Edward Sewter
June 22	Thomas s. of Daniel White
Oct. 17	George s. of Thomas Perry
Nov. 21	Urslie d. of Urslie Holdway
Jan. 15	Margery d. of Edward Windsor
Jan. 23	Robert s. of John Sandle
Feb. 1	Robert s. of John Legge
Feb. 27	John s. of William Ryole

1631.

Mar. 27	Mary d. of Edward Sewt'
April 22	Lucie d. of Henry Edwards
April 27	Samuel s. of John Lambe
July 10	John s. of John Cuffe
July 10	William s. of Laurence Rolles
Nov. 14	William s. of Richard Smith
Dec. 31	Joane d. of Robert Ryole ye younger
Jan. 14	Susan d. of Alexa'der Ada's
Feb. 10	Mary d. of Thomas Smart
Feb. 12	Walter s. of John Sandle
Feb. 15	Robert s. of Robert Joupe
Mar. 18	Nicholas s. of Robert Sheepeheard

1632.

April 29	Dorothy d. of John Davis
May 20	Elizabeth d. of William Holdway
July 2	William s. of William Brickle
Sep. 9	Joane d. of William Brittaine
Oct. 28	Thomas s. of Thomas Perrie
Nov. 13	Marie d. of Thomas Reed
Dec. 9	Agnes d. of Robert Kinnison
Feb. 6	John s. of David White
Feb. 17	Edward s. of William Bernard

Mar. 16 Julian d. of Edward Shuter
Mar. 16 Dorothie d. of Elizabeth Sandlo,
     widdow

1633.

May 1 Henry s. of Henry Edwards
May 8 Francis s. of John Sandle,
     weaver
May 26 Sisely d. of Josias White
July 25 Joan d. of Edward Helier
Aug. 25 Robert s. of Alexander Adams
Oct. 18 John s. of James Pesey
Feb. 9 John s. of Robert Joupe
Feb. 28 Susanna d. of Leonard Snooke
Mar. 2 Dorothie d. of William Hold-
     way
Mar. 16 Peter s. of John Lambe
Mar. 23 Margery d. of Lawrence Rowles

1634.

May 15 Sibyll d. of William Poore
July 7 Richard s. of John Sandle
Aug. 3 John s. of Edward Eton
Nov. 23 Sisely d. of William Bernard
Dec. 24 Edward s. of Robert Shepheard
Jan. 24 Thomasin d. of Robert Ryall
Jan. 28 Anne d. of Thomas Perry
Feb. 18 John s. of Francis Joupe
Mar. 7 Robert s. of John Davis
Mar. 20 William s. of Margaret Combes

1635.

Mar. 26 Edith d. of John Sandle
Mar. 30 Elenor d. of Elenor Ryall
April 10 Alice Shuter d. of Edward
     Shuter
April 19 Emanuel s. of Henry Edwards
April 26 Richard s. of George Greene
May 2 Robert s. of Peter Sandle
July 19 Elizabeth d. of Robert Kenison
Oct. 4 Thomas s. of Thomas Smart
Dec. 6 Walter s. of Robert Joupe
Feb. 25 Edward s. of Edward Helier
Feb. 2 Elizabeth d. of Josias White
Mar. 9 Peter s. of James Pesy

1636.

Mar. 28 John s. of John Sandle
April 3 William s. of William Holdway
April 18 Jane d. of John Lambe
May 1 Joane d. of Edward Windsor
May 15 John s. of Alexander Adams
June 19 Nicholas s. of Thomas Perry
Sep. 29 John s. of John Sandle
Nov. 16 Francis s. of Robert Joupe
Nov. 16 Katherine d. of Robert Davis
Nov. 20 Peter s. of Peter King
Nov. 21 Elizabeth d. of Anne Combes

Nov. 20 John s. of Nathaniel Field,
     Parson
Mar. 1 Walter s. of Thomas Reade
Mar. 3 Joane d. of Edmund Ludlow

1637.

May 7 Peter s. of Peter Sandle
May 28 Elizabeth d. of Lawrence Rowles
June 4 George s. of Henrie Edwards
June 18 Anne d. of Walter Brittaine
July 8 Alice d. of Edward Helier
July 19 William s. of Francis Joupe
Dec. 24 Jane d. of John Davis
Dec. 26 Sarah d. of Edward Shuter
Jan. 14 Joseph s. of William Poore
Mar. 4 Roger s. of Roger Stile
Mar. 16 Susanna d. of Thomas Smart

1638.

Mar. 26 George s. of John Euill
Mar. 29 Anne d. of Peter King
Mar. 30 Robert s. of Robert Ryall
April 22 Marie d. of James Pesey
April 29 Edith d. of William Holdway
     & Solina
Nov. 18 Joane d. of Alexander Adams
     & Magdalene
Feb. 3 Richard s. of Josias White &
     Elizabeth
Feb. 17 Mary d. of Thomas Tabor &
     Joane

1639.

April 17 William s. of George Greene &
     Mary
April 21 Peter s. of Valentine Pitnie &
     Elenor
May 26 Anne d. of Mr Thomas Cox &
     Jane
May 26 Edmund s. of Robert Toope &
     Katherine
Oct. 20 William s. of Robert Joupe &
     Anne
Nov. 17 Elizabeth d. of John Davis &
     Elizabeth
Jan. 5 Susan d. of Margaret Combes
Feb. 9 Elizabeth d. of Andrew Grimes
     & Maude
Feb. 19 John s. of John Euill & Mary

1640.

Mar. 29 Basill d. of Robert Davis &
     Katherine
April 6 Henrie s. of Eame Ryall
May 10 Dorothie d. of Peter King &
     Joane
May 10 Isaak s. of Robert Shepheard
     & Elenor

May 11 Francis s. of Francis Joupe & Margaret

May 31 Thomasine d. of John Sandle & Thomasine

June 10 Elizabeth d. of John White & Edith

July 19 Edward s. of Edward Shuter & Julian

Sep. 13 Robert s. of William Holdway & Solina

Sep. 20 Mary d. of William Poore & Marie

Sep. 24 William s. of Robert Sandle & Elizabeth

Nov. 8 David s. of Robert Toope & Katherine

Dec. 30 John s. of Thomas Stone & Marie

Jan. 10 Marie d. of Thomas Gapper & Marie

Jan. 17 Mathew s. of Mathew Combes & Elizabeth

Jan. 31 Arthur s. of Arthur Sangar & Dorothie

1641.

April 7 John s. of John Preslie & Margerie

May 30 John s. of John Rodway & Alice

July 11 Edith d. of Henrie Edwards & Susan

July 27 Dorothie d. of Alexander Adams & Magdalene

Sep. 5 John s. of James Pesey & Joane

Sep. 12 Rachel d. of Roger Stile & Elizabeth

Oct. 24 Margaret d. of Robert Joupe & Anne

Nov. 7 Thomas s. of Thomas Tabor & Joane

Dec. 27 Edith d. of James Stroud & Edith

Jan. 19 Jane d. of Edward Helier & Alice

Jan. 30 Anne d. of Andrew Grimes & Maude

Feb. 20 Elizabeth d. of Robert Sandle & Elizabeth

Feb. 27 Edward s. of Edward Simmes & Dorothie

Mar. 30 Margaret d. of Francis Joupe & Margaret

1642.

May 31 Francis s. of Thomas Stone & Marie

June 12 John s. of Thomas Perrie & Margaret

June 16 Steven s. of Steven Bradden & Anne

June 26 Jane d. of George Greene & Mary

July 24 Mary d. of Peter Sandle & Mary

July 29 William s. of John Euill & Mary

Aug. 28 Richard s. of Margaret Combes

Oct. 30 Marie d. of Thomas Banister & Marie

Dec. 5 Jane d. of John Welch & Jane

Dec. 11 Francis d. of Mr John Freake & Marie

Dec. 21 Thomas & Francis sons of John Rodway & Alice

Jan. 5 William s. of Robert Toope & Katherine

Jan. 22 Peter s. of William Poore & Marie

Jan. 25 Elizabeth d. of James Pesey & Joane

Jan. 29 Marie d. of Cutbert Willmot & Marie

Mar. 17 Elizabeth d. of Edward Shuter & Julian

1643.

April 3 Alice d. of Robert Jaques & Alice

May 7 Mary d. of James Stroude & Edith

May 30 Alexander s. of Robert Davis & Katherine

July 13 Elizabeth d. of Mathew Combes & Elizabeth

Oct. 8 Anne d. of Thomas Gapper & Marie

Dec. 2 Marie d. of Alexander Adams & Magdalene

Dec. 27 Philip s. of Mr John Freake & Marie

Jan. 12 Dorothie d. of William Inges & Elizabeth

Feb. 28 Roger s. of John Davis & Elizabeth

1644.

May 5 Robert s. of Thomas Tabor & Joane

May 5 Alice d. of Roger Stile & Elizabeth

July 5 Richard s. of Richard Younge & Susan

July 5 Joan d. of John Welch & Jane

Sep. 24 Elizabeth d. of Mr Nathaniel Field & Rachel

c

Oct. 13   Joane d. of Mary Allford
Nov. 1   Robert s. of Francis Joupe & Margaret
Nov. 24   Elenor d. of John Rodway & Alice
Jan. 5   Anne d. of Thomas Banister & Marie
Jan. 5   Edward s. of Marie Sandle
Jan. 19   John s. of John Erill & Marie
Feb. 3   Elizabeth d. of Robert Toope & Katherine
Mar. 9   Marie d. of Thomas Perrie & Margaret
Mar. 23   John s. of Peter Sandle & Mary

1645.

April 11 Jane d. of John Welch & Jane
April 27 Cuthert s. of Cutbert Willmot & Marie
June 29   Elizabeth d. of John Legate & Thomasine
July 21   Bridget d. of Mr John Freake & Marie
Aug. 17   Anne d. of Edward Dowdin & Anne
Aug. 3   Winefride d. of William Inges & Elizabeth
Sep. 14   Mary d. of Richard Younge & Susan
Sep. 14   Jane d. of Thomas Stile & Edith
Nov. 2   Susan d. of George Harding & Dorothie
Nov. 16   John s. of James Stroude & Edith
Dec. 7   George s. of George Greene & Mary
Dec. 21   John s. of Edward Shuter & Julian
Jan. 4   Joane d. of Robert Davis & Katherine
Feb. 22   John s. of Mr John Slatford & Grace
Feb. 26   Mary d. of Thomas Stone & Mary
Mar. 8   Richard s. of Rachel Chanell

1646.

Mar. 30   Mathew s. of Mathew Combes & Elizabeth
April 14 Deborah d. of Nicholas Lawrence & Cecill
June 24   Grace d. of Thomas Gapper & Marie
Aug. 2   Robert s. of Robert Jaques & Alice
Oct. 18   William s. of Robert Shepheard & Elenor

Oct. 25   Elizabeth d. of Manuel Swetman & Grace
Nov. 1   Susanna d. of William Poore & Marie
Dec. 20   Richard s. of Thomas Hunt & Florence
Jan. 22   Thomas s. of Robert Toope & Katherine
Feb. 14   Marie d. of Edward Shuter & Julian
Feb. 24   Joane d. of John Bradden & Marie
Mar. 7   William s. & Elizabeth d. of John Presly & Margerie

1647.

Mar. 28   Christopher s. of Alexander Adams & Magdalene
April 20 Thomas s. of Richard Younge & Susan
May 13   Philip d.* of Philip Guppill & Mary
May 16   Susanna d. of Robert Sandle & Elizabeth
Aug. 15   Jane d. of John Smart & Katherine
Sep. 26   Richard s. of John Enill & Marie
Nov. 7   Sarah d. of Thomas Banister & Marie
Nov. 28   Henrie s. of Cutbert Willmot & Marie
Dec. 9   Anne d. of Margaret Combes
Jan. 2   John s. of Francis Jonpe & Margaret
Jan. 9   William s. of Thomas Stile & Edith
Jan. 16   Elizabeth d. of John Rodway & Alice
Jan. 16   Joane d. of Margaret E . . es
Mar. 15   Elizabeth d. of Roger Stile & Elizabeth

1648.

Mar. 26   Edward s. of Thomas Hunt & Florence
April 9   Ambrose s. of Ambrose Hill & Margaret
April 23 James s. of Peter Sandle & Marie
April 30 John s. of John Welch & Jane
June 3   Richard s. of Mr Nathaniel Field & Rachel
June 11   Thomasine d. of James Stroude & Edith
June 11   John s. of William Poore & Marie

* So in original.

July	9	Thomas s. of George Harding & Dorothie
Sep.	17	Joane d. of Robert Toope & Katherine
Nov.	12	Mary d. of Mathew Combes & Elizabeth
Dec.	17	John s. of John Trimboy & Anne
Jan.	8	Marie d. of William Edwards & Lucie
Jan.	25	Joane d. of Robert Jaques & Alice
Feb.	4	Elizabeth d. of Richard Younge & Susan
Feb.	15	William s. of William Pereman & Marie
Mar.	11	Willm s. of Cristpher Winsor & Mari*

1649.

April	29	Thomas s. of Edward Gibbes & Elizabeth
May	18	Francis s. of Francis Cuffe & Basill
Aug.	11	Elizabeth d. of John Bradden & Marie
Sep.	18	Edmund s. of Edmund Swetnam & Jone
Oct.	17	Elizabeth d. of Mr John Freake & Marie
Dec.	12	Thomas s. of Thomas Stile & Edith
Dec.	26	John s. of John Cornish & Jane
Mar.	10	Edith d. of John Rodway & Alice

1650.

April	21	Nathaniel s. of John Euill & Marie
May	19	William s. of Alexander Adams & Magdalene
July	7	Jane d. of Cutbert Willmot & Marie
July	7	Susanna d. of Richard Younge & Susan
Jan.	5	Jane d. of William Edwards & Lucie
Jan.	19	Robert s. of Robert Toope & Katherine
Feb.	16	John s. of James Stroude & Edith
Mar.	2	Manuell s. of Edmund Swetnam & Jone
Mar.	14	Valentine s. of Valentine Bradden & Joane

* Interlined in a very bad hand.

1651.

[blank]		Elinor d. of Thom. Banister*
July	3	Susanna d. of William Poore & Marie
July	17	Jane d. of Jolliffe Toogood & Joane
Aug.	24	Marie d. of William Rowles & Christian
Aug.	26	John s. of Mr John Freake & Mary
Aug.	31	Dorothie d. of George Harding & Dorothie
Sep.	7	Anne d. of Mathew Combes & Elizabeth
Sep.	14	Susanna d. of John Smart & Katherine
Sep.	14	William s. of William Whitcombe & Sarah
Oct.	19	John s. of Thomas Stile & Edith
Oct.	26	Robert s. of Robert Greene & Alice
Jan.	8	Susanna d. of Thomas Hunt & Florence
Jan.	18	Dinah d. of Peter Sandle & Marie
Feb.	15	John s. of Manuel Swetman & Grace
Feb.	22	John s. of John Bradden & Marie
Mar.	4	Mathew s. of Cristper Winsor & Mari†

1652.

April	12	Richard s. of Francis Cuffe & Basill
May	3	John s. of Edmund Swetman & Joane
June	20	Joane d. of Richard Younge & Susan
July	4	Anne d. of Thomas Wadly & Anne
Sep.	16	Francis d. of Mr Charles Croke & Marie
Nov.	4	Christian d. of John Trimboy & Anne
Jan.	7	Sisely d. of John Rodway & Alice
Jan.	16	John s. of William Edwards & Lucie
Feb.	15	Robert s. of Mr John Freake & Marie
Mar.	20	Alexander s. of Robert Greene & Alice

* Interlined in a different hand.
† Interlined in the same bad hand as 1648.

1653.

Mar. 27	Dorothe d. of Thomas Banister & Marie
April 30	Jane d. of Valentine Bradden & Joane
June 19	Susanna d. of John Humphries & Susanna
Aug. 16	John s. of Thomas Hunt & Florence
Aug. 28	Charles s. of Charles Davis & Sisely
Sep. 18	Francis s. of Alexander Adams & Magdalen
Oct. 9	Roger s. of Thomas Stile & Edith
Oct. 30	Rachel d. of Mr Charles Croke & Marie
Oct. 31	Cristoper s. of Cristopher Winsor & Mari*

1654.

June 28	Bartholomew s. of John Bradden & Marie
July 16	Abraham s. of Edmund Swetman & Joane
Aug. 2	Judith d. of Mathew Combes & Elizabeth
Aug. 24	Beniamin s. of Manuel Swetman & Grace
Jan. 10	Joane d. of James Stroude & Edith
Jan. 16	William s. of William Smart & Michael
Feb. 27	Anne d. of John Trimboy & Anne
Mar. 4	Jane d. of John Humphries & Susanna
Mar. 19	William s. of John Welch & Jane

1655.

Mar. 27	Charles s. of Mr Charles Croke & Marie
April 8	Elizabeth d. of Charles Davis & Sisely
April 14	John s. of Mr John Freake & Marie
Dec. 14	Abraham s. of Edmund Swetman & Joane
Jan. 27	Edward s. of William Edwards & Lucie
Feb. 8	William s. of William Smart & Michael
Mar. 12	John s. of Robert Greene & Alice
Mar. 24	Joseph s. of Cristopher Winsor & Mari*

* Interlined in the same hand as before.

1656.

June 2	Elizabeth d. of George Harding & Dorothie
June 5	Susanna d. of Edward Edwards & Marie
June 6	John s. of Steven Jefferies & Elizabeth
Oct. 17	Francis s. of Manuel Swetman & Grace
Nov. 5	Susanna d. of Thomas Stile & Edith
Nov. 16	Edmund s. of Robert Ryall & Alice
Nov. 16	Joane d. of Richard Yonng & Susan
Nov. 28	John s. of Valentine Bradden & Joane
Dec. 7	Alice d. of John Doggerell & Thomasine
Feb. 15	Francis d. of Charles Davis & Sisely
Feb. 22	Elenor d. of John Rowles & Sibylla
Mar. 1	William s. of Francis Cuffe & Basill
Mar. 9	Lucie d. of Mr John Freake & Marie
Mar. 9	Elizabeth d. of Mr Charles Croke & Marie

1657.

Mar. 28	Robert s. of William Smart & Michael
June 16	John s. of John Rodway & Alice
July 3	Jane d. of George Tite & Susan
Aug. 16	Thomas s. of Peter Sandle & Marie
Sep. 1	Dorothe d. of Mathew Combes & Elizabeth
Sep. 15	Charles s. of John Euill & Marie
Jan. 19	Jonah s. of William Parfoote & Marie
Feb. 26	Elizabeth d. of John Trimboy & Anne

1658.

April 4	William s. of William Edwards & Lucie
May 8	Margaret d. of John Tabor & Rose
May 13	Robert s. of William Smart & Michael
May 20	John s. of George Harding & Dorothe

Aug. 15	Marie d. of Edward Edwards & Marie
Aug. 15	William s. of Robert Greene & Alice
Oct. 21	Jane d. of Richard Young & Susan
Nov. 27	George s. of John Edwards & Avice
Jan. 23	Basill d. of John Smart & Katherine
Jan. 29	Elenor d. of Valentine Bradden & Joane
Feb. 20	Marie d. of Charles Davis & Sisely
Feb. 23	Edward s. of Timothie Sandle & Christobell

1659.

Jan. 18	Henry s. of Mathew Stowrton & Brigit
May 12	Rachel d. of John Humphries & Rachel
June 3	Roger s. of James Stroud & Edith
July 17	Abraham s. of Rice Griffith & Jane
Dec. 27	Thomas s. of Edmund Swetman & Joane
Jan. 22	William s. of William Statham & Susan
Jan. 22	Marie d. of John Tabor & Rose

1660.

April 1	Thomas s. of Robert Ryall & Alice
May 1	Joan d. of Matthew Combes & Elizabeth
Aug. 5	John s. of John Rowles & Sibylla
Sep. 14	Elizabeth d. of William Parfoot & Marie
Nov. 1	Jane d. of Charles Davis & Sisely
Nov. 19	Dorothe d. of William Smart & Michael
Dec. 15	Elizabeth d. of John Humphries & Rachel
Dec. 23	Jane d. of John Bernard & Marie
Jan. 24	Marie d. of John Joup & Marie
Feb. 4	Anne d. of Edward Edwards & Marie

1661.

May 26	George s. of Robert Greene & Alice
July 18	Katherine d. of Mr Charles Croke & Marie

Aug. 9	John s. of Valentine Bradden & Joane
Aug. 29	Thomas s. of Timothie Sandle & Christobell
Nov. 5	Alice d. of John Smart & Katherine
Nov. 27	James s. of Matthew Combes & Elizabeth
Jan. 26	Ruth d. of John Edwards & Avice
Feb. 23	Katherine d. of Charles Davis & Sisely

1662.

April 3	Basill d. of Francis Cuffe & Basill
April 19	William s. of Robert Ryall & Alice
May 26	Marie d. of Edmund Swetnam & Joane
June 15	Henrie s. of Henrie Jefferies & Susan
Oct. 28	Timothie s. of Timothie Sandle & Christobell
Feb. 5	Edward s. of William Parfoote & Marie
Mar. 17	Anne d. of Francis Hunt

1663.

Aug. 30	George s. of Edward Edwards & Marie
Sep. 13	Anne d. of John Bernard & Marie
Oct. 28	John s. of John Joup & Marie
Nov. 8	Joane d. of Edmund Moxam & Jane
Nov. 25	Robert s. of Robert Joup & Melior
Jan. 28	Thomas s. of Thomas Gartrell & Marie

1664.

April 11	Anne d. of William Parfoote & Marie
July 17	George s. of Renaldo Monke & Dorothie
Aug. 3	Edward s. of Henrie Jefferie & Susan
Aug. 15	Edith d. of Robert Ryall & Alice
Aug. 16	Marie d. of Valentine Bradden & Joane
Oct. 20	Richard s. of Richard Chinocke & Jane
Nov. 26	Henrie s. of William Edwards & Lucie
Dec. 11	John s. of John Edwards & Anice

Dec. 18   Sisely d. of Charles Davis & Sisely

Dec. 31   Richard s. of Richard White & Marie

Feb. 22   John s. of Robert Feltham & Marie

1665.

Mar. 29   John s. of Edward Baker & Edith

June 18   Francis s. of John Joup & Marie

Aug. 6   Elizabeth d. of William Pennie & Elizabeth

Nov. 12   Richard s. of Richard White & Marie

Dec. 6   Christobell d. of Timothie Sandle & Christobell

Dec. 24   Edward s. of Edward Edwards & Marie

Mar. 18   Marie d. of Robert Goden & Grace

June 1   Thomas s. of Thom. Wilkins & Hellen*

June 24   Edward s. of William, Lord Stourton, & Elizabeth*

1666.

April 16   Sarah d. of John Bernard & Marie

April 29   Jane d. of Robt Green & Alee

May 4   Robert s. of Robert Davis & Francis

May 28   Jane d. of Edmund Swetnam & Joane

June 24   Jone d. of Willm Parfet & Marie

Oct. 24   Renaldo & John sons of Renaldo Monke & Dorathi

Nov. 27   John s. of John Smart & Katherine

Dec. 10   Thomas s. of Robert Riall & Alee

Dec. 23   Mari d. of Richard Chenocke & Jane

Jan. 10   Joane d. of Valentine Bradden & Joane

Feb. 21   Elizbeth d. of Willm Sandall & Elizbeth

1667.

Mar. 29   Francis s. of Mathew Stourton & Brigit†

April 1   Francis s. of Tho. Wilkins & Hellen†

* These two entries interlined in another hand.

† These two entries interlined.

May 12   John s. of Charles Davis & Siseli

June 6   Mari d. of James Scote & Mari

June 14   Thomas s. of William, Lord Stourton, & Elizabeth*

July 14   William s. of John Jupe & Mari

July 21   Margret d. of Robt Greene & Alee

Aug. 14   Francis s. of Edward Baker & Edeth

Aug. 29   Jane d. of Henri Jefri & Susan

Jan. 12   Mari d. of Richard White & Mari

Jan. 16   Mari d. of Mr Thomas Jhons & Jane

Feb. 5   John s. of Timothi Sandall & Cristable

Mar. 10   Willm s. of Margret Jupe

Mar. 15   John s. of Edward Edwards & Mari

Mar. 23   Paule s. of Peter Sandall & Caterne

1668.

June 14   Edward s. of Willm Meadon & Sarah

July 19   Sarah d. of Robt Goden & Grace

Sep. 22   Anne d. of Willm Parfet & Mari

Sep. 27   John s. of John Adams & Mari

Feb. 2   Mari d. of John Jupe & Mari

Dec. 13   Robert s. of [blank] Tabor & Tomeson

1669.

Mar. 28   Mari d. of Robert Davis & Francis

July 24   Anne d. of Thomas Wilkins & Hellen†

Sep. 5   Thomas s. of Robt Greene & Alee

Sep. 5   Elizabeth d. of Nicholas Bowne & Mari

Oct. 22   John s. of John Barnard & Mari

Oct. 24   Willm s. of Robt Feltham & Mari

Oct. 31   Willm s. of Charles Davis & Sesili

Nov. 14   Alee d. of James Meadon & Alee

Nov. 4   Charles s. of William, Lord Stourton, & Elizabeth†

* Written on the margin in another hand.

† Interlined in another hand.

Nov. 25	Catherne d. of John Smart & Catherne
Dec. 5	Francis s. of Richard White & Mari
Dec. 12	Edmund s. of John Sheppd & Joane
Jan. 25	Rachell d. of John Hart & Dorethi
Feb. 13	Robert s. of Edward Baker & Edeth
Mar. 3	Ann d. of Henri Jefri & Susan

1670.

June 17	Robrt s. of Robrt Riall & Alee
Nov. 7	John s. of John Presli & Ann
Feb. 22	John s. of Edward Suter & Mari
Mar. 21	Caterne d. of Willm Parfit & Mari

1671.

June 7	Joseph s. of John* White & †
June 13	Mari d. of Willm‡ Meadon & Sarah
Sep. 24	Robrt s. of John Jupe & Mari
Jan. 21	James s. of James Medon & Alee
Feb. 4	Josias s. of Richard White & Mari
Feb. 15	Elizabeth d. of Timothi Sandall & Cristable

1672.

April 12	John s. of Willi. Evill & Marg.
May 16	Alexander s. of Alex. & Elizabeth Dyer
June 7	Grace d. of Edward & Edith Baker
Sep. 12	Mary d. of Jane Braden, base b.
Sep. 20	John s. of Rob. & Tomasin Tabor
Oct. 7	Willi. s. of Willi. & Mary Maidman
Oct. 20	Ambrose s. of John & Katharine Smart
Nov. 4	Charles s. of Rob. & Fracis Davis
Nov. 17	Willi. s. of Willi. & Christian Otbor
Dec. 1	Thom. s. of John & Mary Barnot
Dec. 21	Jane d. of Willi. & Rose Style
Jan. 7	Rachel d. of Charles & Syeilly Davis

Mar. 21	Willi. s. of John & Mary Adams
Mar. 23	Bassill d. of John & Joane Sheapard

1673.

April 13	James s. of James & Ann Pease
April 22	Mary d. of Robert & Mary Feltham
July 27	John s. of John & Ann Presly
Aug. 10	Elizabeth d. of Robert & Elizabeth Toope
Oct. 25	Mathew s. of John & (?)* Heart
Dec. 21	Jane d. of Willi. & Sarah Meaden
Mar. 10	John s. of John Drew, Rector, & Dorathy
Mar. 20	Susan d. of John & Susan Poore

1674.

July 24	John s. of John & Joane Joupe
Aug. 30	Mary d. of John & Joane Sheapard
Sep. (?)	Mary d. of Willi. & Mary Maidman
Sep. 20	Elizabeth d. of John & Avis White
Sep. 24	Mary d. of Richard & Mary Reed
Nov. 25	Robert s of Richard & Susanna Atkins
Nov. 29	John s. of William & Mary Evill
Dec. (?)	Sarah d. of Robert & Mary Adams
Jan. 11	Robert s. of George & Elizabeth Green
Feb. 26	Thomas s. of Tim. & Christable Sandall
Mar. 21	Robert s. of Richard & Mary White

1675.

May 14	John s. of Alexander & Elizabeth Dyer
Aug. 1	Judith d. of Charles & Cyeily† Davis
Sep. 18	Mary d. of Richard & Edith Evill
Oct. 1	Michaell d. of William & An Brimson
Oct. 24	Margery d. of John & Jone Joupe

---

* *Richard* written first and struck out.
† *Mari* written and struck out.
‡ *Edward* written first and struck out.

* The name has been altered and is illegible; it should be *Dorothy*, cf. 1675 and 1677.
† In D. R. Eliz.

Nov. 24	Thomas s. of Robinn* & Tomasin Tabour		Sep. 26	Hanah d. of William & Mary Evill
Feb. 13	Mary Hart d. of John & Dorathy		Oct. 16	John s. of Robert & Tomsin Tabor*
Mar. (?)	Bassill d. of John & Catharine Smart		Nov. 1	Elizab. d. of Alixander & Elizabeth Dyer
			Dec. 1	Mary d. of Steeven & Elizabeth Owen

1676.

April 9	Elizabeth d. of John & Jone Gerrett		Dec. 11	Mary d. of John & Mary Joupe
April 27	Thomas s. of John & Ann Presly		Jan. 18	Elizabeth & Mary ds. of John & Ann Pery†
June 9	Willi. s. of John & Susan Poore		Jan. 20	William s. of William & Sarah Meaden
July 23	Francis s. of Robert & Mary Felthome		Feb. 13	William base s. of Ann Banister
Aug. 27	Gertrude s.† of William & Hannah Joupe		Feb. 15	Richard s. of Richard & Susan Atkins
Nov. 16	Katharine d. of Will. & Mary Evill		Mar. 18	Walter s. of John & Dorathy Hart
Nov. 24	Susannah d. of Rich. & Susan Atkins		Mar. 22	Martha d. of Matthew & Sarah Lucas
Nov. 26	Elizabeth d. of Eliz. & George Green			
Dec. 30	Jane d. of John & Ann Perry			**1679.**
Dec. 31	Katharin d. of John & Joane Sheapard		April 9	Dorathy d. of William & Bridgett Brashaw‡
Mar. 12	William s. of John & Abigall Butcher		April 26	Francis s. of John & Margery Evill

1677.

[blank]	John s. of Richard & Mary White		May 7	Margarett d. of John & Susan Poore
May 11	Francis s. of John & Dorothy Heart		May 18	William s. of Robert & Hannah Toope
Aug. 12	Thomas s. of Thomas & Phillis‡ Barnet§		May 23	Francis s. of William & Hannah Joope§
Aug. 19	Sarah d. of Mathew & Sarah Lucas		June 14	Mary d. of John & Avis White
Oct. 26	John s. of Robert & Grace Goden‖		June 17	Isaake s. of John & Katharine Sheapard
Nov. 21	John & Peter sons of John & Susan Poore		July 13	William s. of William & Joane Raynelds
Dec. 6	Thomas s. of Richard & Edith Evill		Sep. 7	James s. of Walter & Ann Sparrow
Dec. 23	William s. of William & Ann Brimson		Nov. 3	Francis s. of Robert & Mary Joope§
Feb. 11	Elizabeth base d. of Joane Bradden		Dec. 4	Rich. s. of Robert & Mary Felthom
Mar. 17	Margaret d. of Charles & Sisily Davis		Dec. 21	Thomas s. of William & Ann Brimson
			Jan. 1	Rachell d. of Alexander & Elizabeth Dyer
	1678.		Jan. 1	Mellior d. of John & Joan Sheapard
April 18	Ann d. of Tim. & Christible Sandall		Jan. 4	Elizabeth d. of Edmond & Lucy Sweatman
			Feb. 21	William s. of George & Elizabeth Green

* In D. R. Robert. † So in original.
‡ Mary written first and struck out.
§ In D. R. Barnard. ‖ In D. R. Goodwin.

* This entry is not in D. R.
† In D. R. Pearcy; vide Burials, 1678.
‡ In D. R. Brausher. § In D. R. Joupe.

1680.

June 13 Thomas s. of Robert & Sarah Godden
June 17 Henry s. of Henry & Susan Foote
June 20 Mary d. of Mary & John Pearcy
Aug. 1 John s. of John & Elizabeth Owen
Aug. 11 Mary d. of Mary Adams, base borne
Aug. 14 Mary d. of William & Mary Evill
Aug. 22 Mary d. of Robert & Fracis Davis
Sep. 2 Charles s. of Richard & Edith Evill
Sep. 27 Robert s. of Timothy & Christible Sandall
Oct. 3 William s. of Richard & Mary White
Nov. 25 Joane d. of William & Jane Duffit
Dec. 27 John s. of William & Mary Maidment
Feb. 26 Abigall d. of John & Abigall Bucher

1681.

Jan. 10 Ann d. of Tho. & Jane Mayo

[There is half a page in the original Register left blank here, and in the D. R. there are no transcripts for several years hereabouts.]

1682.

Sep. 6 John s. of John & Joue Sheapard, at Barrow
Sep. 7 Matthew s. of Thomas Tope
Oct. 11 Jerome s. of Jerome & Mary Parfitt
Nov. 1 Robert s. of Robert & Grace Godden
Nov. 25 Joane d. of John & Dorathy Hart
Dec. 29 Mary d. of John & Joue Poore
Jan. 18 William s. of William & Hannah Joupe
Feb. 23 Mary d. of Robert & Mary Joupe

1683.

May 3 Rueth d. of William & Sarah Meaden
July 1 John s. of Robert & Francis Davis

July 16 Thomas s. of William & Mary Sheapard
Aug. 5 Rachell Wild d. of Daniell Wild, of Shasbury
Aug. 27 Sarah d. of William & Mary Evill
Aug. 28 John s. of William & Jane Du-thought
Aug. 13 Jaell d. of John Joupe & Elizabeth
Sep. 16 Annis d. of William Maidment
Sep. 13 Elizabeth d. of Steeven & Ann Owen
Oct. 12 William s. of William & Mary Barnett
Dec. 2 John White s. of John & Alce White
Jan. 8 Elizabeth Atkins d. of Richard & Susan Atkins
Jan. 9 William s. of John & Elizabeth Evill
Jan. 13 Charity d. of John & Margarett Sparrow
Mar. 3 Elizabeth d. of John & Mary Percy
Mar. 7 John s. of Frances* & Ann Sweatman
Mar. 15 Katharine d. of Robert & Hannah Toope

1684.

April 17 Elizabeth d. of John & Abigall Bucher
May 24 Ann d. of Thomas & Sarah Wadly, of Froome Selwood, aged 7 years
May 24 Mary d. of Thomas & Sarah Wadly, of Froome Selwood, aged 2 years
Nov. 28 Mathew s. of Richard & Mary White
Nov. 30 Katharine d. of Rich. & Edith Evill
Nov. 30 Hannah d. of Rob. & Hannah Green
Jan. 1 Ann d. of John & Joane Sheapard
Feb. 2 Cycily d. of John & Dorathy Hart

1685.

April 26 [blank] of William & Ann Brimson
June 11 Sarah d. of Thomas & Sarah Wadly

* *John* written first and struck out.

Aug. 9   Ann d. of William & Mary Evill

Oct. 5   Elizabeth d. of John & Dorathy Heyter

Oct. 13   William s. of William & Jane Duthought

Oct. 30   Robert s. of Robert & Rose Ryall

Nov. 16   Nicholas s. of John & Abigall Bucher

Jan. 21   Francis s. of John & Elizabeth Joupe

Feb. 6   John s. of William & Mary Barnett

Mar. 15   Mary d. of Robert & Margaret Feltham

1686.

April 7   Ann d. of Edward & Joyce Royall

April 11   John s. of John & Mary Walter

May 4   Elizabeth d. of John & Elizabeth Evill

June 13   Matthew s. of Lawrence & Judith Butt

Aug. 29   Edith d. of John & Jane Strowd

Sep. 7   William s. of John & Dorathy Hart

Sep. 22   Katherine d. of Robert & Hannah Toope

Nov. 24   Robert s. of Steeven & Ann Owen

Nov. 30   Richard s. of William & Ann Perman

Dec. 28   John s. of John & Margaret Sparrow

Jan. 23   Bassill d. of John & Joane Sheapard

Feb. 18   James s. of William & Jane Duffitt

1691.*

April 1   Chatherine d. of John & Jane Edwards

April 26   Catherine d. of John & Catherine Picford

Aug. 1   Mathew s. of William & Mary Barnett

Aug. 16   John s. of Robert & Ann Owen

Aug. 26   Catherine d. of Paul & Sarah Sandall

Sep. 13   John s. of William & Ann Perman

* There is a gap from 1687, when the first book ends, to 1691, when the next book begins.

Oct. 12   George s. of Robert & Hannah Green

Nov. 1   Joane d. of Edmond & Lucy Sweatman

Jan. 24   Mary d. of John & Elizabeth Evill

Feb. 2   Mary d. of William & Ann Davis

Feb. 19   James s. of James & [blank] Dredge

Feb. 22   Maurice s. of John & Mary Walter

Mar. 24   Joseph-Davis Barber s. of Jo. & Abigall Barber

1692.

April 8   John s. of William & Elizabeth Beamond

May 16   William s. of William & Jane Duffitt

July 24   John s. of William & Alce Edwards

Aug. 5   John s. of Edward & Anastatia Edwards

Aug. 30   Elizabeth d. of Richard & Elizab. Moores

Sep. 15   Jane d. of William & Rueth Smith, of Kiln.[ington]

Oct. 18   Dorathy d. of John & Dorathy Hart

Nov. 23   Ann d. of Steeven & Joane Owen

Jan. 1   Henry s. of John Baker & Jone

Jan. 11   Mary d. of Robert & Ann Owen

Jan. 15   John s. of John & Jane Edwards

Jan. 23   James s. of James & Jane Meaden

Feb. 27   Thomas s. of John & Alce White

Mar. 4   Richard s. of John & Jone Shepard

Mar. 24   John s. of William & Alce Lamber

1693.

April 18   Mary d. of Andrew & Mary Turner (?)

Aug. 20   Tabitha d. of John & Mary Walter

Aug. 27   Benjamin s. of John & Abigall Butcher

Sep. 3   William s. of William & Elizabeth Frieth

Sep. 12   John s. of William & Jane Green

Sep. 20   John s. of James & Elizab. Dredge

Oct. 22	Jerome s. of Edward & Grace Edwards
Mar. 18	Mary d. of William & Ann Perman
Mar. 24	Jane d. of William & Jane Duffit

1694.

April 22	Jane d. of Frances & Ann Sweatman
May 15	Willi. s. of Willi. & Elizabeth Beamon
Aug. (?)	Samuel s. of John & Abigall Bueher
Sep. 17	Uriah s. of James & Elizabeth Dredge
Dec. 2	Mary d. of James & Mary Meaden
Dec. 7	Willi. s. of Christopher Targett & Mary
Dec. 11	John s. of Jo. & Elizabeth Joupe
Jan. 25	Paul s. of Robert & Margaret Feltham
Feb. 17	Joane d. of John & Jone Baker
April 5*	Mary d. of William & Mary Edwards

1695.

April 5	Mary d. of William & Alce Edwards
April 30	John s. of Cooke & Eith
May 27	Will. s. of Rich. & Elizab. Moores
June 2	Ann d. of John & Mary Walter
June 7	Steeven s. of Steven & Joane Owen
Sep. 8	George s. of George & Elinor Edwards
Oct. 13	Elizab. d. of Rob. & Ann Owen
Dec. 8	Moses s. of William & Alce Lamber
Dec. 22	Joannah d. of Will. & Reuth Smith
Dec. 31	Samuel s. of Christopher & Mary Targett
Feb. 3	Mary d. of Thomas & Mary Ryall
Feb. 13	John s. of John & Elizab. Evill
Mar. 16	George s. of John Edwards
April 25	Mary d. of Giles & Elinor Joupe

1696.

Sep. 16	William s. of John Feltham & Miriam

Sep. 20	John s. of Jael Clement & Elizabeth
Nov. 20	Mary d. of William Beamond & Elizab.
Dec. 19	Elizab. d. of Mary & Math. Combs
Jan. 10	Mary d. of John Barber & Abigall
Feb. 8	Elizab. d. of James Dredge & Elizab.
Mar. 23	Thomas s. of Thomas Cooke & Edith

1697.

April 5	Giles s. of William Perman & Ann
June 13	Robert s. of John Baker & Jone
June 20	John s. of Rich. Pinnolds & Martha
July 12	Elizab. d. of William Dun & Elizab.
Aug. 2	Ann d. of Rich. Lappain & Francis
Sep. 19	Elinor d. of George Edwards & Elinor
Mar. 8	Tiu. s. of Thomas Sandall & Francis
Mar. 12	Nicholas s. of John Barber & Abigall

1698.

July 5	Robert s. of William Miles
Aug. 7	William s. of William & Edith Bugden*
Aug. 24	Sarah d. of John White
Aug. 28	Rueth d. of Rich. Moore
Sep. 4	Elinor d. of Giles Joupe*
Sep. 25	James s. of William Lamber*
Oct. 13	John s. of Robert & Ann Owen
Feb. 5	James s. of Paul Sandall
Mar. 9	Thomas s. of Thomas & Mary Ryall

1699.

April 5	George s. of William Beamond
April 10	James s. of John & Joan Baker
May 28	Richard s. of John & Rueth Hill
June 4	William s. of John & Jane Edwards
July 23	Mary d. of John & Mary Smart
July 30	Martha d. of Steeven & Jone Owen

* So in original.

* In D. R. these entries are erased.

1700.

April 11	George s. of George Moore & Jane*
April 12	Elizab. d. of Thomas Sandall
May 31	Lucy d. of William & Mary Miles
June 16	Charles s. of William & Alce Edwards
June 30	Mary d. of George & Elinor Edwards
Sep. 20	Valentine s. of William Duffit
Oct. 27	Isit d. of John & Isit Michell
Jan. 1	George s. of George Rools, of Kilming.[ton]
Jan. 6	Sarah d. of John Heyter, of Sailes [Zeals]
Feb. 2	Martha d. of Rob. Feltham
Feb. 4	Ann d. of George & Elizab. Gilbert
Mar. 2	Edward s. of Giles Joupe
Mar. 2	Mary d. of James Kaines

1701.

April 13	Thomas s. of William King & Mary
July 13	Elioner d. of Robert & Ann Owen
Sep. 1	John s. of Rich. & Rachell Atkins
Oct. 12	Willi. s. of John & Mary Smart
Nov. 8	William s. of Elizab. Sweatman, base borne
Nov. 9	Francis s. of John & Jone Baker
Nov. 12	Elizab. d. of Rich. & Elizab. Moore
Feb. 1	Joan d. of Thomas & Mary Ryall
Feb. 15	William s. of William & Ann Frip

1702.

April 30	Jane d. of William & Mary Miles
May 9	Mary d. of William & Sarah Meaden
May 29	Mary d. of John Feltham & Miriall†
Sep. 17	John s. of Thom. & Francis Sandall
Nov. 2	Sarah d. of Hugh & Sarah Heyter
Nov. 7	Elizab. d. of Rich. & Rachel Atkins

* In D. R. this entry is omitted.
† In D. R. Miriam.

Nov. 17	Mary d. of James & Lucy Meaden
Nov. 29	Rich. s. of John & Jane Edwards
Dec. 13	Will. s. of Willi. & Melliar Jenkins
Dec. 14	Tho. s. & Joan d. of Steeven & Elizab. Smith
Feb. 8	Davenish s. of Davenish & Eliz. Sheane
Mar. 10	Ann d. of John & Margarett Holly

1703.

April 9	Thomas s. of Thomas & Joane Tabor
July 4	Cicily d. of Charles & Jane Evill
Aug. 12	Dorathy d. of John & Issett Michel
Aug. 15	Elizab. d. of Elizabeth Green, base borne
May 3	Walter s. of Walter & Eliz. Barnes*
Sep. 19	Henry s. of William & Mary Miles
Nov. (?)	Rich-Gay s. of Mr John Maddox, of Kilmington
Dec. 2	Elizabeth d. of George & Elinor Edwards
Dec. 5	Bassell d. of John & Mary Smart
Jan. 19	Joane d. of John & Jone Baker
Feb. 27	Alce d. of John & Mary White

1704.

Mar. 30	Elizabeth d. of James & Luce Meadon
May 13	John s. of Mr John & Mrs Dorothy Drew
May 15	Stephen s. of Stephen & Elizabeth Smith†
June 5	John s. of Thomas Lapham & Hannay, Kilmington†
June 6	William s. of William & Melior Jenkins
June 15	David s. of Mary Morly, bas.†
July 2	Robert s. of Francis & Ann Baker
July 16‡	John s. of George & Eliz. Gilbert
July 27	Joan d. of Thomas & Joan Tabor

* Interlined by another hand; omitted in D. R.
† Omitted in D. R.
‡ The date of this entry in D. R. is Oct. 30.

July 30 Richard s. of Difnesh & Eliz. Shean

Aug. 13 Ann d. of Robert & Ann Owen*

Sep. 3 Robert s. of Walter & Eliz. Barnes†

Sep. 10 Edith d. of John & Mary Herniman, of Kilmington*

Oct. 3 Jonathan s. of Will. & Sarah Meadon*

Oct. 16 Joan d. of Rich. & Eliz. Moore

Oct. 22 Will. s. of Will. & Rebeckah Barnet

Oct. 26 Susannah d. of Hugh & Sarah Hater

Nov. 11 Rich. s. of Rich. & Rachel Atkins

Nov. 26 Thomas s. of Tho. & Eliz. Parett‡

1705.

Mar. 27 John s. of John Holly & Margaret

April 12 Thomas s. of Tho. & Frances Sandell

April 22 John s. of John & Ann Shuter

Sep. 9 Sarah d. of Mary Owen, base

Nov. 1 Thomas s. of Rich. & Mary Brinall, of Broham

Dec. 18 Edward s. of Mr John & Mrs Dor. Drew

Jan. 1 Charles s. of Will. & Rebeckah Barnet

Feb. 15 Edward s. of John & Jane Edwards

Mar. 3 Mary d. of Tho. & Joan Tabor

1706.

April 10 John s. of John & Iset Michel

May 6 Frances d. of Will. & Ann Davis

June 9 Charles s. of Charles & Jane Evil

Sep. 15 Frances d. of John & Mary White

Sep. 28 Grace d. of Will. & Ann Skreen

Oct. 5 Mary d. of Francis & Susanna Jupe

* Omitted in D. R.
† Omitted in D. R., and interlined in original.
‡ Omitted in D. R. The following entries are added in D. R., but without dates:
  Baptized by Papist Priest.
  Robert s. of Walter Barnes & Elizth
  Mary d. of John & Mary Sheapard
  Francis d. of Francis Wall & Hen.

Nov. 13 Mary d. of John & Ann Shuter

Nov. 26 Thomas s. of Robert & Ann Owen

Dec. 16 Mary d. of Jonathan & Ruth Mullens

Dec. 27 John s. of William & Mary Miles

Feb. 26 John s. of Hugh & Sarah Hayter

Mar. 19 Thomas s. of John & Margaret Holly

1707.

May 4 James s. of Robert & Lucy Owen

May 17 Mary d. of Peter & Mary Gover

May 28 Joseph s. of James & Sarah Cains

Aug. 2 James s. of Francis & Ann Baker

Aug. 10 James s. of John & Joan Baker

Aug. 11 Ann d. of Samuel & Ann Lambe

Sep. 5 Sarah d. of William & Sarah Meadon

Oct. 5 Robert s. of John & Mary Smart

Nov. 5 James s. of Thomas & Joan Tabor

Dec. 6 Alice d. of Thomas & Mary Ryall

Jan. 26 Charles s. of William & Ann Davis

1708.

April 27 Edward s. of George & Ellenour Edwards

Aug. 5 Mary d. of Willm & Rebeccah Barnet

Aug. 19 Charles s. of Charles & Jane Evile

Oct. 12 Anne d. of Stephen & Mary Penny

Nov. 4 Martha d. of John & Miriam Feltham

Nov. 10 Joseph s. of John & Margaret Holly

Nov. 14 Mary d. of Richd & Eliz. Moore

Dec. 27 Elizabth d. of Robert & Eliz. Tabor

Jan. 3 Walter s. of Hugh & Sarah Hayter

Feb. 7 Cecilia d. of Tho. & Cecilia Green

Feb. 21 George s. of Mr John & Mrs Dorothy Drew

1709.

Mar. 25	Mary d. of Mathew Mawbam, Travler
May 22	Ruth d. of Peter & Mary Gover
May 24	Ruth d. of John & Mary Green
Sep. 8	Francis s. of Francis & Susanna Jupe
Oct. 6	William s. of Willm & Rebeckah Lamb
Oct. 16	John s. of Robt & Eliz. Alford
Nov. 13	Ellen d. of Willm & Mary Reynolds
Nov. 13	William s. of James & Sarah Cains
Nov. 15	John s. of Tho. & Joan Tabor
Dec. 28	Basil d. of John & Mary White
Jan. 6	John s. of John & Mary Ransome
Feb. 19	James s. of Willm & Sarah Meadon

1710.

June 25	Mary d. of Robt & Lucy Owen
Aug. 27	Jerome s. of Willm & Mellior Jenkins
Oct. 3	William s. of William & Anne Davis
Oct. 22	John s. of Benjamin & Mary Gullifer
Oct. 28	Richard s. of Richard & Hannah Ingram, of Brewham
Nov. 26	Anne d. of William & Rebeccah Barnet
Jan. 24	Hannah d. of Will. & Mary Coward, of Gillingham
Mar. 3	Mary d. of Charles & Jane Evile

1711.

Oct. 4	Stephen s. of Stephen & Mary Penny
Oct. 19	Mary d. of Samuel & Ann Lamb
Dec. 10	Thomas s. of Tho. & Cecilia Green
Dec. 28	Honour d. of John & Mary Green
Jan. 28	Mary d. of John & Sarah Barnet
Feb. 3	Rachel d. of Tho. & Mary Smith, of Zeals
Feb. 13	Mary d. of Eliz. Gilbert
Feb. 27	Mary d. of Richard & Mary Skreen, of Zeals
Mar. 20	Susanna d. of Francis & Susanna Jupe
Mar. 22	Charles s. of Peter & Mary Gover

1712.

Mar. 27	Mary d. of Willm & Mary Jupe
April 14	William s. of John & Mary Bucher
April 18	Elizabeth d. of Steph. & Mary Collins
April 29	John s. of John & Mary Bradden
May 11	Anne d. of Mary Owen, bas.
May 18	William s. of Will. & Mary Reynolds
June 19	Thomas s. of Tho. & Elizabeth Ridgley
July 3	Mary d. of John & Mary White
July 23	William s. of John & Mary Evil
July 24	George s. of Mr John & Mrs Dorothy Drew
Oct. 1	Rebeckah d. of W^m & Rebec. Lamb
Jan. 10	Agnes d. of Thomas & Joan Taber
Feb. 16	Robert s. of Robert & Elizabeth Tabor
Feb. 22	John s. of John & Sarah Barnet
Mar. 4	Thomas s. of John & Mary Ransom

1713.

April 3	Bridget d. of Robt & Lucy Owen
April 12	Charles s. of Ben. & Mary Gulliffer
April 16	Mary d. of James & Sarah Cains
April 16	Thomas s. of Thos & Elizabeth Gatehouse
April 20	Patience d. of Robt & Elizabeth Alford
April 22	Susannah d. of John & Miriam Feltham
May 20	Basil d. of Thos & Margery Hurdle
Aug. 2	William s. of Joan Lewis, bas.
Oct. 12	Will. s. of Charles & Jane Evile
Nov. 6	Rich^d s. of Will. & Rebecca Barnet
Jan. 4	John s. of John & Dulcina Trimby
Jan. 15	John s. of William & Mary Joup
Feb. 15	John s. of John & Joan Baker
Mar. 1	Samuel s. of Samuel & Ann Lamb

1711.

Mar. 29   Susannah d. of Francis & Susannah Joup

April 24   Thomas s. of Thomas & Dorcas Swain

April 29   Jane d. of Henry & Mary Cooper

June 4   Ann d. of William & Mary Meaden

June 20   Elizabeth d. of Thomas & Mary Ryal

Sep. 15   Stephen s. of John & Mary Bradden

Oct. 2   Robert s. of Richard & Rachel Atkins

Oct. 3   Joan d. of John & Mary Green

Nov. 2   Ann d. of William & Patience Michel

Dec. 13   Dionysia d. of John & Ann Shepherd

Feb. 27   Ann d. of John & Rebecca Markey

1715.

Mar. 29   Catharine d. of John & Catharine Fisher

April 3   Hannah d. of Thomas & Elizabeth Gatehouse, of Gillingham

April 9   Eliz. d. of Charles & Jane Evile

Sep. 18   Edward s. of John & Joan Baker

Sep. 24   James s. of the Honble Charles Sturton & Catharine

Oct. 15   John s. of Robt & Elizabeth Alford

Nov. 15   Mary d. of Richard & Mary Feltham

Dec. 18   Ann d. of Thomas & Dorcas Swain

Dec. 27   John s. of Charles & Catharine Evile

Jan. 4   William s. of William & Bridget Green

Jan. 11   John s. of Thomas & Margery Hurdle

Jan. 12   Hannah d. of William & Mary Joup

Feb. 24   Mary d. of John & Catharine Deacons

Mar. 24   Mary d. of John & Ruth Feltham

1716.

April 7   Abraham & Jacob sons of James & Sarah Cains

April 17   Thomas s. of Stephen & Mary Collins

May 4   Hannah d. of John & Sarah Barnet

May 8   William s. of Stephen & Mary Penny

June 15   Rachel d. of Edward & Rachel Edwards

July 29   Mary d. of Ben. & Mary Gullifer

Aug. 4   Jane d. of Samuel & Ann Lamb

Nov. 10   Jane d. of Charles & Ruth Feltham

Dec. 18   John s. of John & Ann Shepherd

Dec. 28   Jane d. of Willm & Amy Rowles, of Kilminton

Jan. 10   Henry s. of William & Sarah Meadon

Jan. 20   William s. of Francis & Susan. Joup

Jan. 20   Mary d. of John & Mary Edwards

Jan. 28   Elizabeth d. of Robert & Lucy Owen

Mar. 24   Mary d. of John & Mary Ransom

1717.

April 8   Jane d. of John & Catharine Fisher

June 18   Susanna d. of George & Eliz. Phillips

Sep. 26   Robert s. of John & Joan Baker

Oct. 27   John s. of John & Catharine Deacons

Oct. 28   Edith d. of Charles & Catharine Evile

Dec. 30   James s. of William & Mary Markey

Dec. 31   John s. of Thomas & Dorcas Swain

Feb. 27   Jane d. of William & Edith Frith

1718.

April 28   Joseph & Mary s. & d. of Robt & Elizabeth Alford

May 17   Thomas s. of William & Rebecca Barnet

July 7   Jane d. of Charles & Jane Evile

Oct. 19   Grace d. of Edward & Rachel Edwards

Nov. 15   John s. of Richard & Mary Feltham

Dec. 23 Mary d. of Charles & Catharine Évile

Jan. 8 Luce d. of Thomas & Margery Hurdle

Feb. 2 Samuel s. of John & Mary Edwards

Feb. 5 James s. of James & Dorothy Sandal

Feb. 8 William s. of William & Elizabeth Scammel

Feb. 29 Henry s. of Robert & Lucy Owen

1719.

April 2 Robt s. of Richard & Rachel Atkins

April 14 Eliz. d. of Robert & Elizabeth Baker

May 21 James s. of John & Mary Bradden

May 24 John s. of John & Ann Target

June 16 Mary d. of William & Mary Markey

June 22 John s. of George & Eliz. Philips

July 5 Eliz. d. of William & Eliz. Brimson

July 11 John s. of John & Ann Shepherd

July 19 Sarah d. of John & Sarah Barnet

Aug. 6 Joan d. of John & Joan Baker

Sep. 9 Henry s. of Henry & Mary Edwards

Mar. 3 Bridget d. of William & Bridget Green

1720.

April 17 James s. of William & Edith Frith

May 5 Joan d. of Robt & Eliz. Baker

July 10 Richard s. of John & Catharine Fisher

July 19 Mary d. of James & Dorothy Sandall

Sep. 1 Basil d. of Francis & Susannah Joup

Sep. 19 James s. of Mr John & Dorothy Drew

Oct. 1 William s. of Charles & Jane Evile

Oct. 11 William s. of John & Catharine Deacons

Nov. 27 James s. of John & Ann Target

Jan. 23 Martha d. of Edward & Rachel Edwards

Feb. 7 Sarah d. of John & Mary Edwards

Feb. 19 Eliz. d. of William & Mary Markey

1721.

May 7 Edith d. of Charles & Catharine Eville

June 23 Catharine d. of John & Catharine Orchard

Aug. 6 Mary d. of Edith Cook, bas.

Aug. 20 Eliz. d. of Thos & Eliz. Ridgley

Oct. 15 Thomas s. of Thomas & Dorothy Spink

Oct. 15 Mary d. of John & Joan Baker

Jan. 1 Hannah d. of Robert & Hannah Falles

Feb. 25 Mary d. of John & Sarah Barnet

Mar. 4 Eliz. d. of Robert & Eliz. Alford

1722.

Mar. 25 William s. of William & Mary Markey

Mar. 27 Elenour d. of Robert & Eliz. Baker

April 9 Thos s. of John & Ann Shepherd

June 29 Ann d. of John & Ann Target

Aug. 19 Martha d. of Nathaniel & Mary Ireson

Mar. 8 Eliz. d. of James & Eliz. Lambert

1723.

June 7 Mary d. of Samuel & Alice Target

June 19 Mary d. of John & Ann Edwards

July 27 John s. of William & Sarah Meaden

Sep. 8 Mary d. of Ann Newton, bas.

Sep. 21 Elisha s. of James & Dor. Sandal

Oct. 10 William s. of John & Joan Baker

Oct. 11 Martha d. of George & Eliz. Edwards

Dec. 1 John s. of Henry & Jane Perfect

Dec. 6 Joseph s. of Thos & Dorothy Spinks

Dec. 14 Mary d. of John & Mary Owen

Feb. 6 Sarah d. of James & Eliz. Lambert

Feb. 7 Margaret d. of John & Ann Target

Feb. 17 Valentine s. of George & Eliz. Phillips

Mar. 1	John s. of Will. & Mary Markey
Mar. 8	Margaret d. of Tho⁸ & Mary Mores, of Gillingham
Mar. 13	Jane d. of Nathaniel & Mary Ireson

1724.

May 31	Susan'a d. of Joseph & Han'ah Stone
Aug. 28	Mary d. of John & Mary Ireson
Aug. 30	Mary d. of George & Elizabeth Edwards
Feb. 7	George s. of Henry & Mary Edwards
Feb. 7	Susan'a d. of John & Ann Edwards
Mar. 18	Joan d. of Samuel & Alice Target

1725.

Mar. 29	Thomas s. of James & Dorothy Sandle
Aug. 16	Edward s. of John & Ann Target
Aug. 17	Henery s. of Henery & Jane Perfect
Oct. 18	Mary d. of Nathaniel & Mary Ireson
Nov. 17	Richard s. of John & Joan Baker
Jan. 19	William s. of Will⁵ & Sarah Bond
Jan. 28	Jane d. of Tho⁸ & Dorothy Spinks
Feb. 16	Martha d. of Will⁵ & Edith Feltom
Feb. 17	William s. of Will⁵ Bratcher
Feb. 18	Ann d. of Charles & Catharine Evil
Mar. 17	Martha d. of Charles & Ruth Feltom

1726.

May 19	George s. of John & Catharine Deacons
May 29	Mary d. of Will⁵ & Mary Combs
June 26	John s. of John & Mary Owen
July 10	Philip s. of William & Mary Markey
Dec. 26	John s. of Will⁵ & Edith Frith
Feb. 10	Basil d. of George & Elizabeth Green

Feb. 15	John s. of William & Eleanor Heytor, of Mere
Mar. 10	Abigail d. of John & Mary Ireson
Mar. 16	Charity d. of Ann Shepherd, base born

1727.

April 6	William s. of Richard Lapham
April 10	John s. of Charles & Dorothy Evil
May 11	John s. of Samuel & Alice Target
May 22	Martha d. of John & Ann Target
May 24	George s. of George & Elizabeth Edwards
June 13	Sarah d. of William & Sarah Bond
June 14	John s. of John & [blank] Webb
July 12	Charles s. of Edw⁴ & Basil Edwards
July 13	Ann d. of John & Ann Edwards
July 31	Mary d. of Rob⁵ & Dorothy Miles
Oct. 10	William s. of Stephen & [blank] Owen
Nov. 26	Martha d. of Martha Owen, base born
Jan. 6	Robert & Richard sons of Hen⁷ Parfect, of Mere
Jan. 24	Margery d. of John & [blank] Walter
Feb. 11	Joseph s. of [blank]*
Mar. 17	Stephen s. of Joseph & Han'ah Stone

1728.

May 14	Mark s. of Mark & Mary Snellgrove of yᵉ parish of [blank]
June 9	William s. of Charles & Catharine Evil
June 29	Jane d. of Robert & Elizabeth Goddin†
July 2	Thomas s. of Charles & Dorothy Evil
July 14	Shadrack s. of Will⁵ & Edith Frith
July 25	Mary yᵉ unbaptized d. of John & Catherine Williams, born‡
Sep. 6	Matthew s. of Will⁵ & Eleonar Heyter

* Omitted in D. R.
† Before this entry there is " June 23 . . . d. of Robert . . . . Arnold " struck out.
‡ Interlined : omitted in D. R.

E

Oct. 30	Mary d. of John & Ann Target	
Nov. 1	Ann d. of John & Mary Owen	
Nov. 17	John a base born s. of Philis Cooper	
Nov. 28	George s. of George & Elizabeth Green	
Dec. 20	Martha base born child of Elizabeth Web*	
Jan. 4	Martha d. of yᵉ Revᵈ Mʳ John & Mʳˢ Grace Hill	
Mar. 22	John s. of John & Frances Trowbridge	

1729.

April 19	William s. of Edward & Basil Edwards
May 11	Margaret d. of Abraham & Ann Butt
July 13	Prusella d. of William & Prusella Edwards
Sep. 12	William s. of Robert & Dorothy Miles
Oct. 12	Honour d. of Samuel & Alice Target
Nov. 29	Thomas s. of Henery & Jane Cooper
Jan. 23	Sarah yᵉ unbaptized d. of John & Catharine Williams,born†
Feb. 22	George s. of James & Francis‡ Arnold
Feb. 24	William s. of Charles & Catharine Evil
Mar. 11	John s. of John & Ann Edwards

1730.

Mar. 30	Ann d. of Charles & Dorothy Evil
May 25	Roger s. of Roger & Ann Hilleker
June 29	Catharine d. of Richard Lapham
Aug. 25	Robert s. of George & Eliz. Edwards
Oct. 12	William s. of Henery & Melior Brim'ing, of Bourton
Nov. 7	Betty d. of Wᵐ & Sarah Bond
Dec. 22	William s. of George & Elizabeth Green
Jan. 23	Rose d. of William & Eleoner Heyter, of Mere
Feb. 11	John s. of William & Ann Bratcher
Feb. 17	John s. of John & Ann Wilkins
Feb. 27	Ann d. of Mark & Mary Snellgrove

* Omitted in D. R.
† Interlined; omitted in D. R.
‡ James and Francis omitted in D. R.

1731.

Mar. 28	Hannah d. of John & Mary Owen
Mar. 30	John yᵉ unbaptized s. of John & Catharine Williams, born*
May 7	James s. of James & Ann Whitaker
May 24	John s. of Richard & Mary Edwards
May 25	Charles s. of Edward & Basil Edwards
May 27	Henery s. of the Revᵈ Mʳ John & Mʳˢ Grace Hill
Aug. 30	William s. of William & Joan Smart
Sep. 24	John s. of John & Frances Trowbridge, of East Knoile
Dec. 20	Thomas s. of John & Sarah Walter
Feb. 27	Ann d. of James & Frances Arnold

1732.

[blank]	Sarah d. of Henery & Jane Cooper, near this time*
April 23	Ann d. of Joseph & Han'ah Stone
April 24	Elizabeth d. of Henery & Margaret Miles
May 25	John s. of Robert & Jane Smart
July 31	John s. of Roger & Ann Hilliker
Aug. 1	Mary d. of Jonathan & Rachel Meaden
Aug. 25	Betty yᵉ unbaptized d. of John & Catharine Williams, born*
Sep. 26	Ambrose s. of Robert & Hannah Fallis
Oct. 2	Thomas s. of Robert & Dorothy Miles
Oct. 9	Hannah d. of Charles & Dorothy Evil
Oct. 12	Ann d. of John & Mary Edwards
[blank]	George s. of George & Elizabeth Green
Nov. 25	Thomas s. of Richard & Elizabeth Arnold
Dec. 14	Joan d. of William & Edith Feltom
Dec. 29	Eleonar d. of Francis & Eleonar Jupe

* Interlined : D. R. deficient.

1733.

Mar. 26	Mary d. of William & Eleonar Heytar
April 23	Mary d. of Edward & Basil Edwards
April 24	Martha d. of Samuel & Alice Target
July 15	Thomas s. of John & Ann Target
July 22	Drew s. of Mark & Mary Snellgrove
July 29	James s. of ye Revd Mr John & Mrs Grace Hill
Aug. 17	Betty d. of Charles & Catharine Evil
Aug. 26	William s. of William & Ann Bradshaw, *alias* Bratcher
Oct. 7	Hannah base born d. of Mary Meaden
Nov. 1	Richard s. of James & Frances Arnold
Dec. 13	Richard s. of Edmund & Mary Wadloe
Nov. 23	Thomas s. of William & Susan'a Mores
Jan. 26	Thomas ye unbaptized s. of John & Catharine Williams born*
Jan. 31	Mary d. of Robert & Jane Smart

1734.

May 3	William s. of William & Betty Andrews
May 15	George s. of Richard & Eleonar Bratcher
Aug. 4	William s. of John & [*blank*]† Target
Aug. 10	Francis s. of John & Mary Hull, of Stower Provost
Sep. 15	Ann d. of James & Jane Meaden
Nov. 4	Susan'a d. of Francis & Eleonar Jupe
Nov. 10	Jane d. of John & Mary Owen
Nov. 14	James s. of Richard & Mary Edwards
Nov. 20	William s. of John & Joan Top
Dec. 15	Grace d. of William & Eleonar Heyter
Dec. 26	Patience d. of William & Mary Markey
Dec. 26	James s. of Henery & Jane Cooper

* Interlined : D. R. deficient.
† In D. R. Hannah.

Jan. 19	Jane d. of John & Mary Edwards
Feb. 12	William s. of Richard & Elizabeth Arnold

1735

Mar. 25	William s. of William & Susan'a Mores
April 20	Thomas s. of James & Frances Arnold
April 28	James s. of James & Jane Baker, of Bourton
May 7	Elishua d. of Samuel & Alice Target
May 25	Catharine ye unbaptized d. of John & Catharine Williams, born*
June 25	Robert s. of Robert & Dorothy Miles
Aug. 17	Flower d. of Michael & Ann Lapham, of Killmington
Aug. 28	William s. of Richard & Eleonar Bratcher
Oct. 30	Thomas s. of Thomas & [*blank*] Combs
Nov. 9	John s. of Edward & Basil Edwards
Jan. 1	Sarah d. of Joseph & Han'ah Stone
Jan. 1	Bridget d. of Robert & Jane Smart
Jan. 1	Betty d. of James & [*blank*] Cleeves, of Kilmington
Jan. 28	Ann d. of John & Joan Top
Feb. 11	John s. of James & Mary Taber
Feb. 15	Elizabeth d. of John & Mary Jackson

1736.

April 2	Charles s. of Thomas & Mary Taber
April 27	Elizabeth d. of Robt & Han'ah Vallis
May 15	Bartholomew s. of William & Mary Edwards
May 25	John s. of William & Susanna Mores
May 29	Philip base born child of Jane Miles
June 20	Mary d. of James & [*blank*] Bull
Oct. 26	Elias s. of James & Jane Meaden
Nov. 19	Samuel ye unbaptized s. of John & Catharine Williams, born*

* Interlined : omitted in D. R.

Jan.   6   Michael s. of Jonas & Ann
           Brimson, of Killmington
Jan. 17   Betty d. of Robert & [blank]
           Turner
Jan. 18   Betty d. of Francis & Eleonar
           Jupe
Feb. 23   Mary d. of Joseph & Mary
           Holly (being Ash Wednes-
           day)
Feb. 23   Jane d. of John & [blank]
           Mitchel, of Killmington
Mar.   6   Mary d. of Ruth Moores, base
           born
Mar. 16   William s. of William &
           Eleonar Heyter
Mar. 22   John s. of William & [blank]
           Lapham, of Killmington

1737.

April 13   James s. of James & Mary
           Taber
May   2   Sarah d. of John & Jane Par-
           sons, of Kilmington
May   17   Rose d. of Walter & Rebecca
           Alford
May   20   Susanna d. of ye Revd Mr John
           & Mrs Grace Hill
May   25   Martha d. of George & Eliza-
           beth Edwards
June   2   William s. of Mary Crembe,*
           base born
June 23   Martha d. of Richard & Mary
           Edwards
Sep. 10   Mary d. of Samuel & Mary
           Hordinet, of Gare Hill in
           the parish of Froom
Sep. 12   Mary d. of William & Susanna
           Jupe
Sep. 21   Mary d. of John & Joan Top
Oct. 30   Charles s. of Henery & Jane
           Cooper
Nov. 24   Alice d. of Samuel & Alice
           Target
Dec. 11   Sarah d. of James & Ann
           Baker
Dec. 21   Susanna d. of William & Sus-
           anna Mores
Dec. 25   Joanna d. of Robert & Jane
           Smart
Feb. 14   John s. of Thomas & Elizabeth
           Ridgley
Feb. 26   Mary d. of John & Hannah
           Target
Feb. 28   Mary d. of James & Joan
           Sanger, of Mere

* Perhaps Crombe, as in D. R. See Marriages,
1737.

1738.

April 7   Jane d. of Edward & Basil
           Edwards
April 30   Thomas s. of William & Mary
           Markey
July 16   Charles base born s. of Joan
           Baker
Aug.   1   Samuel s. of James & Ann
           Whitaker
Oct. 15   Sarah d. of James & Frances
           Arnold
Oct. 16   Lizeth d. of John & Mary
           Mitchel, of Kilmington
Nov. 26   Mary d. of Joseph & Ann
           Shean, of Mere
Dec. 17   Thomas s. of [blank] Sutton
Jan.   1   Ann d. of William & Ann
           Bratcher
Jan. 10   Edward s. of Edward Young,
           of Kilmington
Jan. 14   Joshua s. of John & Mary
           Jackson
Jan. 16   Jane d. of Thomas & Mary
           Taber
Jan. 20   Robert s. of James & Mary
           Taber
Jan. 21   Robert s. of George & Eliza-
           beth Green
Jan. 21   Quirina d. of James & Jane
           Meaden
Jan. 22   Betty d. of Richard & Ann
           Atkins, junr
Jan. 29   Mary d. of John Bradden, junr,
           & Elizabeth
Jan. 29   Ann d. of Edmund & Mary
           Wadloe
Feb. 20   James s. of Stephen & Mary
           Bradden
Feb. 20   Sophia d. of Richard & Eleonar
           Bratcher

1739.

April 3   Leonard s. of Robert & Dorothy
           Miles
April 16   William s. of William & Edith
           Feltom
Aug. 18   Betty d. of John & Joan Top
Oct.   4   William s. of John & Hannah
           Laws
Oct.   7   Flower d. of William & Edith
           Heyter
Oct. 14   John s. of Thomas & Elizabeth
           Farthing, of South Brewham
Oct. 20   James s. of William & Mary
           Edwards
Jan. 20   James s. of James Bull

Jan. 20 Elizabeth d. of Walter & Rebecca Alford

Feb. 10 Joshua s. of Richard & Mary Edwards

Feb. 16 Giles s. of William & Susanna Jupe

1740.

May 27 Elizabeth d. of Andrew & Ann Hoskins, of Gillingham

June 7 James s. of James & Ann Baker

June 7 Han'ah d. of Edward & Sibyl Gilbert, of Kilmington

July 21 Basil d. of Edward & Basil Edwards

Oct. 12 Susanna d. of William & Susanna Moores

Dec. 9 Sarah d. of Charles & Mary Gover

Dec. 23 John s. of Stephen & Mary Bradden

Feb. 11 Mary d. of John & Ann Smith, of Head Stocks in Killmington

Feb. 21 Jane d. of Richard & Ann Atkins

Feb. 22 Elizabeth d. of Joseph & Ann Shean, of Mere

Mar. 1 Joanna d. of Thomas & [blank] Urson* (otherwise Harcourt), of Mere

Mar. 8 Mary d. of John & Mary Jupe

Mar. 15 Mary d. of James & Mary Tabor

Mar. 15 Mary Owen, a foundling child

1741.

April 9 Thomas s. of Thomas & Mary Brimson, of Kilmington

April 30 William s. of William & [blank] Perfect, of Zeals

May 31 James s. of Richard & Elizabeth Arnold

July 22 Betty d. of Richard & Susanna Hayward

Aug. 8 John s. of John & Joan Top

Aug. 17 William s. of James & Ann Whitaker

Sep. 12 Ann d. of Joseph & Mary Holly

Sep. 30 William s. of Thomas & Mary Taber

Oct. 18 Edmund s. of John & Hannah Laws

Oct. 21 Thomas s. of John & Sarah Target

* In D. R. Ursin.

Nov. 8 Joan d. of [blank] Clement of Killminton, base born

Nov. 9 John s. of John & Ann Trimby

Nov. 22 John s. of Robert & Dorothy Miles

Feb. 7 James s. of James & Jane Meaden

1742.

Mar. 28 James s. of Richard & Eleonar Bratcher

July 14 Susanna d. of William & Susanna Jupe

Sep. 12 John s. of John & Elizabeth Deacons

Sep. 13 Jane d. of Robert & Jane Smart

Oct. 2 Ann d. of William & Mary Edwards

Oct. 10 Ann d. of George Love, of Kilmington

Nov. 3 James s. of James Smith, of Zeals

Dec. 14 Mary d. of James & Ann Baker

Dec. 19 John s. of John & Jane Edwards

Jan. 2 Molly d. of John & Mary Jackson

1743.

Mar. 26 John s. of Charles & Mary Gover

May 24 Thomas s. of James & Mary Curtis, of Zeals

June 5 Mary d. of John & [blank] Edwards, of W. Knoyle

June 26 Rachel d. of Richard & Ann Atkins

June 30 Ann d. of John & Mary Baker

Sep. 11 Mary d. of Stephen & Mary Bradden

Dec. 25 John s. of Thomas Sutton, of Zeals

Dec. 26 Mary d. of William Lewis, of Zeals

Dec. 27 Mary d. of John & Sarah Target

Jan. 22 Thomas s. of Thomas & Mary Taber

Jan. 29 Ann d. of Robert Smart

Jan. 30 Maurice s. of Maurice & Elizabeth Taswell, of Mere

1744.

Mar. 28 Mary d. of Richard Smith, of Zeals

April 12 Joseph s. of John & Hannah Target

30

April 24	Hannah d. of James & Mary Taber
June 7	Robert s. of William & Susanna Moors
July 21	John s. of James & Ann Baker
Aug. 1	Charles s. of John & Mary Evil
Aug. 14	John s. of William & Edith Feltom
Aug. 22	Susanna d. of John & Ann Lapham
Aug. 31	Catharine d. of John & Joan Top
Oct. 23	Hester d. of Joseph & Mary Holly
Nov. 18	Hannah d. of James & Jane Meaden
Dec. 23	Mary d. of William & Mary Edwards
Dec. 26	Robert s. of Robert & Jane Smart
Jan. 9	Hannah d. of Richard & Mary Edwards
Jan. 19	John s. of Henery & Elizabeth Miles
Mar. 3	Mary d. of Joseph & Rachel Turner
Mar. 6	Elizabeth d. of Robert & [blank] Green
Mar. 8	Betty d. of Elizabeth Deacons, bas.
Mar. 20	Mary d. of John & Elizabeth Bradden

1745.*

April 13	Thomas s. of John & [blank] Dix
May 10	Thomas s. of James Baker, of Bourton
June 8	Peggy d. of Edward & Basil Edwards
July 7	Joan d. of James & Mary Taber
July 20	Richard s. of John & Jane Edwards

* The following entry is written on the fly-leaf of the third Register Book, beginning in 1754, but is given here in accordance with the date:

"Charles Mercator s. of Joseph Walton & Jane his wife was baptized July 25, 1745, o.s., at Brussels in Brabant by the Rev⁴ Montagu Barton, Chaplain to the Royal Regiment of Artillery.

"This Register was transcribed from his Camp Register Book of Christenings, July 12, 1770, by the Rev. M. Barton."

July 23	Mary d. of George Shore, of Yernfield
Aug. 19	Rebecca d. of John & Mary Jackson
Sep. 15	John s. of Morice & Mary Walter
Sep. 21	Peter s. of Charles & Mary Gover
Oct. 14	Mary d. of John Keel, of Brewham
Oct. 25	Diana d. of Samuel & Jane Erbury, of Woolverton in Mere
Oct. 26	Mary d. of Richard & Ann Atkins
Nov. 9	Elizabeth d. of Stephen & Mary Bradden
Dec. 26	John s. of John & Mary Evil
Jan. 25	Elizabeth d. of William & Susanna Jupe
Jan. 29	Mary d. of George & Ann Lapham
Feb. 9	Lyzie d. of William & Abigal Hilleker
Feb. 16	John s. of Thomas & Mary Lampard
Feb. 23	John s. of Richard & Elizabeth Arnold
Feb. 28	Elizabeth d. of John & Jane Parsons, of Kilmington
Mar. 6	Thomas s. of Henery & Honour Edwards

1746.

May 4	Ann d. of Thomas & Sarah Taber
June 1	James s. of John & Sarah Target
June 4	John s. of John & Ann Lapham
June 26	Mary d. of Hannah Laws, base
July 8	John s. of John & Mary Baker
Sep. 24	Rebecca d. of John & Mary Jackson
Sep. 25	Mary d. of John & Ann Trimby
Oct. 19	Betty d. of John & Hannah Target
Dec. 19	Thomas s. of Richard & Eleonar Bratcher
Jan. 18	Samuel s. of James & Basil Hilleker
Feb. 13	Ann d. of James & Ann Baker

1747.

May 11	Jenny d. of Samuel & Mary Arnold, of West Bourton

July 13	Mary d. of Mr William & Mrs Mary Hill
Sep. 6	Elizabeth d. of James & Jane Meaden
Sep. 22	John s. of James & Mary Curtis, of Zeals
Oct. 11	Betty d. of John & Mary Evil
Nov. 1	Thomas s. of Robert & Jane Smart
Nov. 13	Hannah d. of James & Catharine Guire
Nov. 24	Honour d. of William & Susanna Moors
Dec. 7	Mary d. of Matthew & [blank] Combs
Jan. 9	Amona s. of William & Abigal Hilleker
Jan. 24	William s. of William & Mary Edwards
Jan. 31	Thomas s. of Thomas & Sarah Taber
Feb. 2	Thomas s. of Samuel & Ann Edwards
Feb. 9	Robert s. of Richard & Ann Atkins
Feb. 19	Ann d. of Stephen & Mary Bradden
Feb. 26	James s. of Joseph & Rachel Turner
Mar. 21	John s. of John & Elizabeth Bradden

1748.

April 24	Martha d. of Basil Edwards
May 23	William s. of John & Ann Lapham
May 31	James s. of James & Basil Hilleker
June 6	William s. of Issachar & Margaret Farthing
June 29	John s. of Nicholas & Mary Wadlow
July 10	Mary d. of Charles & Mary Gover
July 29	James s. of John Matthews, of Penzelwood
Sep. 4	Ann d. of Hannah Laws, base born
Oct. 3	Hannah d. of Henery & Elizabeth Moors
Oct. 8	George s. of George & Ann Lapham
Oct. 14	Judith d. of Henery Perfect, of Zeals
Oct. 14	Henery s. of Henery & Elizabeth Miles
Nov. 19	Betty d. of James & Susanna Hurry

Dec. 2	John s. of Francis & Mary Faugoin
Dec. 12	Sarah d. of John & Sarah Target
Jan. 3	Mary d. of Samuel & Mary Arnold, of West Bourton
Jan. 18	James s. of John & Ann Trimby
Feb. 6	John s. of John Short, of Brewham
Mar. 10	Edward Parsons s. of Lydia Paps, base born
Mar. 10	Henery s. of John & Elizabeth Hurdle

1749.

June 22	Elizabeth d. of James & Jane Meaden
July 8	Sarah d. of Joseph & Mary Stone
July 28	Phanney d. of Morice & Mary Walter
July 29	William s. of John & Mary Baker
Aug. 26	James s. of Henery & Honour Edwards
Oct. 6	Hannah d. of William & Susanna Moors
Jan. 12	Mary d. of John Perfect, of Zeals
Feb. 18	Charles s. of Thomas Gatehouse, of High Street, Bourton
Feb. 18	Mary d. of John & Mary Evil
Feb. 19	Hanah d. of James & Mary Baily, of Yarnfield, Maiden Bradley
Feb. 22	William s. of Mr William & Mary Hill
Feb. 25	Sarah d. of Richard & Ann Atkins
Mar. 15	John s. of Joseph & Rachel Turner

1750.

Mar. 31	Elizabeth d. of Valentine & Mary Philips
April 4	Ann d. of John & Hannah Target
June 1	Samuel s. of William & Mary Rolls
June 19	John s. of Thomas & Sarah Taber
July 6	Thomas s. of James & Repentance Sanger, of Zeals
July 6	John s. of Edmund & Ann Dowding, of Zeals

July   8   Mary d. of Michael & Ann
            Lapham, of Kilmington
July   30   Martha d. of George & Mary
            Smith, of Zeals
Aug.   28   John s. of Matthew & Betty
            Combs
Aug.   29   Thomas s. of John & Elizabeth
            Bradden
Aug.   30   Edward s. of William &
            Martha Edwards
Sep.   2   Jane d. of James & Ann Baker
Sep.   12   Joseph s. of George & Eliza-
            beth Edwards
Sep.   17   Sarah d. of James & Betty
            Winslow
Oct.   5   Matthew s. of Edward & Eliza-
            beth Turner
Oct.   28   Richard s. of Richard & Ann
            Clement
Oct.   29   Lucy d. of Issachar Farthing,
            of Bourton
Nov.   15   Nathaniel s. of Henery &
            Elizabeth Moors
Nov.   15   Betty d. of Samuel & Mary
            Arnold
Nov.   22   John s. of Philip & Grace
            Markey
Dec.   7   Martha d. of Stephen & Mary
            Bradden
Jan.   31   Hannah d. of John & Sarah
            Target

1751.

April 14   Samuel s. of Charles & Mary
            Gover
May   12   Richard s. of Morice & Mary
            Walter
May   16   Edward s. of Richard & Eleo-
            nar Bratcher
May   23   Charity d. of James & Sus-
            anna Hurry
July   4   Ann d. of Valentine & Mary
            Philips
July   8   James s. of Joseph & Mary
            Stone
Aug.   1   Uriah s. of Samuel & Ann
            Edwards
Oct.   1   Jenny Timer (?) d. of James
            & Han'ah Edwards, of
            Maiden Bradley
Oct.   6   Mary d. of James & Mary
            Curtis, of Zeals
Oct.   16   Mary d. of Nicholas & Jane
            Davidge, of Bourton
Nov.   7   Betty d. of John & Ann
            Lapham
Dec.   30   Mary d. of John & Mary Owen

1752.

Jan.   14   Susanna d. of John & Eliza-
            beth Bradden
Jan.   26   Mary d. of James & [blank]
            Baker, of Bourton
Feb.   16   Robert s. of Thomas & Sarah
            Taber
Feb.   21   Lydia d. of John & Mary Per-
            fect, of Zeals
Mar.   4   Betty d. of William & Martha
            Edwards
Mar.   24   Elizabeth d. of Thomas & Mary
            Evil
April 19   Charles s. of Thomas Gate-
            house, of High Street,
            Bourton
April 19   Sarah d. of James & Jane
            Meaden
May   24   Edward s. of Henery & Honour
            Edwards
July   28   John s. of Mr William & Mary
            Hill
Sep.   17   James & William sons of Rich-
            ard & Ann Atkins
Oct.   9   Martha d. of Henery & Eliza-
            beth Moors
Nov.   9   Fannia d. of John & Mary
            Baker
Dec.   10   Elizabeth d. of William &
            Mary Markey
Dec.   12   Sarah d. of William Edwards
            the thetcher (?)

1753.

Jan.   5   William s. of James & Betty
            Winslow
Jan.   28   Hannah d. of Valentine &
            Mary Philips
Feb.   15   Susanna d. of John & Eliza-
            beth Hurdle
Mar.   7   Rebecca d. of John & Mary
            Owen
April 20   Elizabeth d. of William & Mary
            Rolls
April 20   Samuel s. of Thomas & Eliza-
            beth Rolls, of Killmington
May   13   Mary d. of James & Ann
            Baker
May   31   Joseph s. of Mary Whitaker,
            base born
June   10   Ann d. of John & Sarah Target
Aug.   16   Mary d. of Joseph & Hannah
            Sparrow
Aug.   24   William s. of John & Mary
            Taylor, of Barrow Street
            in Mere
Sep.   24   Merit s. of Thomas & Ann
            Carter, of Zeals

Oct.	7	Elisha s. of George & Han'ah Edwards
Nov.	15	Martha d. of Morrico & Mary Walter
Dec.	16	Sarah d. of Francis & Jane Jupe

1754.

Jan.	7	Mary d. of William & Martha Edwards
Feb.	3	Elizabeth d. of Thomas Gatehouse
Feb.	21	Grace d. of Stephen & Mary Bradden
Feb.	21	John s. of Robert & Mary Green
Feb.	24	Mary d. of Ann Clement. base born
Mar.	1	John s. of William & Han'ah Elliot
Mar.	7	Ann d. of Nicholas & Mary Wadlow
April	7	Betty d. of John & Ann Smith, of Kilmington
April	14	Charles s. of John & Mary Evil
May	19	Susanna d. of John & Ann Trimby
June	2	Richard s. of Charles & Mary Gover
July	1	John s. of William & Mary Rolls
Aug.	26	Sarah d. of George & Ann Lapham
Nov.	3	John s. of John & Eliz. Markey
Dec.	1	Mary d. of Willm & Mary Markey
Dec.	7	Joseph s. of Willm & Eliz. Bond
Dec.	7	Sarah d. of Thos & Sarah Tabor

1755.

Jan.	26	Richard s. of John & Ann Lapham
Feb.	1	John s. of Valentine & Mary Phillips
Feb.	9	Ann d. of William & Ann Edwards
Feb.	12	John s. of John & Eliz. Hurdle
Feb.	16	Mary d. of George & Eliz. Edwards
Mar.	2	Mary d. of James & Jane Meaden
April	13	Phaniah d. of Saml & Ann Edwards
June	29	Martha d. of Jonathan & Eleanor Feltham

Aug.	24	Jane d. of Thos & Phyllis Gittis, from Bourton
Sep.	12	Elisabeth d. of John & Mary Rial
Nov.	5	Grace d. of William & Mary Hill
Nov.	16	Sophia an illegitimate d. of Jane Lapham
Nov.	16	Keziah d. of George & Hannah Edwards
Nov.	21	Ann d. of William & Martha Edwards
Nov.	30	Catherine d. of James & Hannah Stone, from Bourton

1756.

Jan.	18	Elizabeth an illegitimate d. of Jane Godden
Feb.	1	Richard s. of Thomas & Ann Carter, from Zeals
Feb.	15	Mary an illegitimate d. of Patience Markey
Feb.	16	John s. of John & Mary Owen
Feb.	29	Grace d. of John & Mary Tuffin, of Bourton
Mar.	7	Stephen s. of Stephen & Mary Bradden
Mar.	18	Ann Dorothy d. of Montagu & Dorothy Barton
May	12	Phaniah d. of William & Honoria Lapham
May	30	Thomas s. of Richard & Elizabeth Young
July	7	Edmund s. of Nicholas & Mary Wadloe
July	19	Lawrence s. of Lawrence & Grace Cox
Aug.	1	Sarah d. of Matthew & Elizabeth Combs
Aug.	29	Jacob s. of John & Sarah Target
Oct.	5	Margaret a base born d. of Susanna Applegate, of Penn
Oct.	8	Elisabeth d. of William & Ann Edwards
Oct.	10	Hannah d. of George & Ann Lapham
Oct.	10	Mary d. of John & Elisabeth Bradden
Oct.	10	Sarah d. of William & Mary Markey
Oct.	31	Thomas s. of William & Sarah Smart
Nov.	14	George s. of Valentine & Mary Philips
Dec.	13	Mary d. of James & Elizabeth Winsor

F

1757.

Feb. 14 Thomas s. of William & Mary Miles
Feb. 16 Jane d. of John & Eleanor Smart
April 24 William s. of Willm & Eliz^th Bond
May 1 Francis s. of Francis & Jane Jupe
May 23 Mary d. of William & Mary Rowles
May 29 William s. of Thomas & Mary Evile
June 4 Charles s. of Charles & Mary Gover
June 27 Martha d. of Robert & Mary Green
July 10 Betty d. of Thos & Phyllis Gittis, of Bourton
Nov. 6 Charles s. of David & Grace Farthing, of Bourton
Dec. 31 John s. of James & Catherine Luton

1758.

Jan. 15 Martha d. of William & Martha Edwards
Jan. 22 Ann d. of Timon & Sarah Farthing, of Bourton
Jan. 29 John s. of John & Mary Rial
April 9 John s. of Thomas & Sarah Tabor
May 15 John s. of William & Margaret Green
Sep. 10 Joseph s. of James & Catherine Guire
Oct. 1 Elisabeth d. of William & Honoria Lapham
Oct. 15 Mary d. of Valentine & Mary Philips
Nov. 12 Teresa d. of Samuel & Ann Edwards
Dec. 25 George s. of George & Lætitia Bratcher
Dec. 31 Charles & Henry (Twins) s. of Nicholas & Mary Wadloe
Dec. 31 Thomas s. of George & Ann Lapham

1759.

Jan. 14 William s. of William & Sarah Smart
Feb. 11 Ann d. of Thomas & Mary Evile
Feb. 11 Joseph s. of John & Ann Lapham
Mar. 11 James s. of James & Elisabeth Winsor

Mar. 28 Sarah d. of Stephen & Mary Bradden
May 20 James s. of William & Mary Markey
May 21 Charles s. of George & Mary Arnold
June 24 Nanny d. of Matthew & Elizabeth Combes
July 15 William s. of Robert & Grace Edwards
Aug. 5 George s. of Geo. & Mary Tottershall
Aug. 26 Mary d. of W^m & Eliz. Bond
Oct. 4 Catherine d. of Willm & Mary Hill
Oct. 7 Ann d. of John & Mary Rial
Nov. 4 John s. of John & Sarah Target
Nov. 15 Susanna d. of John & Mary Kill, of Brewham Lodge
Dec. 16 William s. of Francis & Jane Jupe

1760.

Jan. 27 Jemima d. of George & Mary Matthews
April 13 Sarah d. of William & Martha Edwards
April 7 Elias s. of William & Margaret Green
April 10 John s. of William & Mary Hillyer
June 1 Keziah an illegitimate d. of Mary Jupe
Sep. 7 Sarah d. of Valentine & Mary Philips
Nov. 9 Mary d. of Robert & Mary Green
Nov. 16 Robert s. of John & Elisabeth Markey, of Zeals

1761.

Jan. 4 Sarah d. of Thomas & Jane Smart, of Kilmington
Jan. 25 Charles s. of William & Honoria Lapham
Feb. 8 Elizabeth d. of Thos & Elizabeth Trimby, of Mere
Mar. 1 Ann d. of William & Sarah Smart
Mar. 29 Hannah d. of John & Mary Rial
April 5 James s. of Robert & Mary Miles
May 17 Ann d. of William & Mary Miles
May 31 William s. of Matthew & Elizabeth Coombs
June 14 George s. of Robert & Grace Edwards

Aug. 16	James s. of Nicholas & Mary Wadloe
Aug. 25	Thomas s. of Thomas & Elizabeth Brimson, of Kilmington
Sep. 27	William s. of William & Mary Markey
Sep. 27	Elizabeth d. of James & Elizabeth Winsor
Oct. 7	Sarah d. of Willm & Elizabeth Bond
Oct. 11	Elizabeth d. of Philip & Ann Miles
Oct. 28	John s. of Benjamin & Mary Rial
Nov. 29	William s. of William & Ann Target
Nov. 29	Mary d. of William & Mary Hillier

1762.

Jan. 10	Mary d. of William & Ann Edwards
Jan. 10	Francis an illegitimate s. of Mary Edwards
Jan. 17	Betty an illegitimate d. of Jane Lapham
Jan. 19	Martin s. of Tho' & Mary Gough, of Penn, Somerset
Jan. 24	Esther d. of Charles & Esther Jefferies, of South Brewham
Feb. 10	James s. of William & Hannah Arnold
Feb. 26	Grace d. of Valentine & Mary Phillips
Feb. 28	Isaac s. of James & Sarah Wilkins
April 15	William s. of John & Elisabeth Hurle
June 6	James s. of William & Margaret Green
June 13	William & Betty (Twins) children of John & Sarah Target
May 24	Susannah d. of John & Elizabeth Rolles
June 20	Charlotte d. of Samuel & Ann Edwards
Oct. 5	Mary d. of John & Sarah Bracher
Nov. 1	Hannah d. of Robert & Mary Miles
Nov. 14	Elizabeth d. of Willm & Ann Target
Nov. 30	William s. of William & Mary Hillier

1763.

Jan. 2	Grace d. of John & Mary Rial
Jan. 26	Joseph s. of William & Sarah Smart
Jan. 23	Elisabeth d. of John & Mary Tuffin, of Bourton, Dorset
Feb. 6	Sarah d. of Robert & Grace Edwards
Feb. 20	Mary an illegitimate d. of Jane Godden
April 17	Isaac s. of Francis & Mary Jupe, of South Brewham
April 27	Charity d. of Thomas & Mary Evil
May 7	William s. of John & Ann Evil
May 25	Dorothy d. of William & Mary Miles
May 30	Edmund s. of George & Mary Arnold
May 30	Ann d. of Charles & Mary Gover
Aug. 28	William s. of Philip & Ann Miles
Sep. 11	Robert s. of Robert & Mary Green
Sep. 25	Betty d. of James & Ann Arnold
Oct. 9	Martin s. of William & Elizabeth Bond
Dec. 26	Ann d. of John & Mary Jefferies

1764.

Jan. 12	Sarah d. of William & Mary Hillier
Jan. 29	Hannah d. of James & Elizabeth Winsor
Feb. 19	Alicia d. of Valentine & Mary Philips
Mar. 1	Thomas & Richard (Twins) s. of Nicholas & Mary Wadlow
Mar. 7	Elizabeth d. of William & Margaret Green
April 8	Charles s. of Charles & Esther Jefferies, of South Brewham
April 29	Silas s. of Charles & Betty Farthing
May 5	Laban s. of William & Honoria Lapham
May 13	Susannah d. of William & Mary Markey
May 27	Mariam d. of William & Ann Target
May 31	Mary d. of John & Hannah Topp

June 10 Thomas s. of William & Mary Rowles

July 1 Leonard s. of William & Mary Miles

July 29 Jane d. of John & Elizabeth Markey, of Zeals

Aug. 7 Susannah d. of John & Mary Rial

Sep. 9 William s. of John & Susannah Gover

Oct. 6 Charles s. of Rob* & Mary Miles

Oct. 21 Nanny the illegitimate d. of Sarah Baker

Nov. 6 Susanna d. of John & Margaret Baker

Dec. 2 John s. of John & Sarah Bratcher

1765.

Feb. 10 James s. of William & Martha Read

Mar. 10 James s. of William & Mary Feltham

Mar. 10 Charles s. of John & Ann Evile

April 22 Robert Griffin s. of William & Ann Hole

May 12 Martin s. of Francis & Mary Jupe, of South Brewham

June 1 Mary d. of Thomas & Mary Evile

June 16 Richard s. of James & Catherine Luton

June 30 Abraham s. of William & Sarah Smart

Aug. 19 Mary d. of James* & Mariam Curtis

Sep. 1 Elizabeth the illegitimate d. of Mary Coombes

Oct. 13 Robert s. of Philip & Ann Miles

Nov. 3 Elias s. of John & Margaret Trimby

Nov. 10 Felix s. of Sam¹ & Ann Edwards

Nov. 24 William the illegitimate s. of Jane Owen

Dec. 8 William s. of John & Mary Rial

1766.

Jan. 5 William s. of James & Ann Arnold

Jan. 5 George s. of William & Margaret Green

Feb. 25 John s. of Thomas & Ann Charlton

* *Thomas* written first and struck out.

Mar. 2 Deletia d. of William & Ann Target

Mar. 2 Susanna d. of William & Betty Target, of South Brewham

May 4 Charlotte d. of James & Elizabeth Winsor

Aug. 4 John s. of Thomas & Patience Trew

Aug. 31 John s. of John & Mary Bradden

Aug. 31 Martin s. of John & Ruth Bishop

Sep. 7 Charlotte d. of John & Ann Jupe

Nov. 19 Keziah d. of William & Honoria Lapham

Nov. 26 James s. of John & Hannah Topp

Dec. 7 Rebecca d. of William & Mary Markey

Dec. 21 William s. of John & Rebecca Burree

1767.

Jan. 8 Mary d. of John & Elizabeth Rolles

Jan. 13 Elizabeth d. of John & Mary Arnold

Feb. 15 Charles s. of Samuel & Mary Arnold, of Zeals

Mar. 30 Felix s. of John & Margaret Baker

April 11 Thomas s. of John & Elizabeth Owen

April 12 Silas s. of James & Susannah Bracher

April 19 Thomas s. of Thomas & Mary Evile

May 3 John s. of Samuel & Ann Edwards

May 5 Thomas s. of Thomas & Ann Charlton

May 9 Marina d. of Robert & Mary Miles

May 17 Esther d. of William & Mary Miles

May 25 James illegitimate s. of Ann Tabor

May 28 Jane d. of William & Margaret Green

June 8 Jane d. of Peter & Christian Gover

June 21 Phaniah d. of Valentine & Mary Phillips

June 21 Mary d. of Robert & Basil Smart

June 21 Edward s. of George & Mary Harsen, of Zeals

July 3 Ann d. of John Albin Shore & Elizabeth, of Whatley, Somerset

Oct. 18 Harry s. of William & Mary Hilliar

Nov. 3 George s. of Thomas & Diana Smart

Nov. 8 Mary d. of John & Ann Talbot, of South Brewham

Nov. 15 Martin s. of William & Ann Target

Nov. 15 William s. of William & Mary Feltham

1768.

Jan. 10 Thomas s. of James & Ann Arnold

Jan. 31 James s. of William & Sarah Smart

Jan. 31 Edward s. of John & Mary Rial

Feb. 17 Joseph s. of Robt & Ann Rial, of Yarnville, Maiden Bradley

April 4 Ann d. of John & Mary Bradden

April 24 Charlotte d. of John & Sarah Bratcher

May 1 Edmund s. of John & Ann Evil

May 8 James s. of John & Margaret Trimby

July 21 James the illegitimate s. of Sarah Moore, of Trowbridge

Aug. 4 Robert the illegitimate s. of Margaret Edwards

Aug. 7 Leah d. of Thos & Mary Evile

Aug. 14 William s. of James & Sarah Whitaker

Nov. 6 John s. of James & Hannah Turner

Nov. 6 John s. of Philip & Ann Miles

Dec. 4 Elizabeth d. of Thomas & Elizabeth Smart, of Seals

Dec. 18 John s. of James & Elizabeth Winsor

1769.

Jan. 15 James s. of John & Esther Miles

Jan. 15 Sarah d. of John & Ann Willis

Jan. 17 William s. of Thomas & Ann Charlton

Jan. 29 William s. of William & Margaret Green

Mar. 6 Abigail d. of Thomas & Sarah Target

April 10 James s. of Thomas & Mariam Curtis

April 16 William s. of Joseph & Grace Elmes

April 30 Hannah d. of John & Ruth Bishop

May 7 Ann d. of John & Jane Edwards

June 4 Esau s. of William & Betty Target, of South Brewham

June 25 Absalom s. of James & Susanna Bracher

July 16 Richard s. of John & Mary Rial

Aug. 6 John s. of John & Hannah Topp

Aug. 13 Isaac s. of William & Sarah Smart

Sep. 24 Hannah d. of James & Mary Baker

1770.

Jan. 7 Thomas s. of John & Margaret Baker

Jan. 18 William s. of Robt & Mary Miles

June 17 Ann d. of Thomas & Elizabeth Tabor

June 24 Leah d. of John & Ann Jupe

July 6 Dinah d. of Thos & Mary Eville

July 25 Jane d. of William & Ann Target

Aug. 3 Edward s. of Thomas & Mary Lampard

Sep. 16 James s. of John & Mary Rial

Sep. 16 Esau s. of John & Ann Evill

Oct. 7 John s. of Joseph & Grace Elmes

Nov. 1 Sandy s. of James & Ann Meaden, of South Brewham

Dec. 9 James s. of John & Mary Bradden

1771.

Jan. 6 Bartholomew s. of Robt & Ann Lapham

Jan. 6 Abigail illegitimate d. of Hannah Philips

Jan. 13 James s. of James & Ann Arnold

Feb. 10 Sarah d. of Thomas & Ann Charlton

Feb. 13 James s. of James & Hannah Turner

Mar. 10 Joseph s. of John & Betty Bird, of Kilmington

Mar. 17 Henry s. of Felix & Alicia Faugoin

Mar. 26 Sarah d. of James & Betty Kaines

April 1 Betty d. of John & Margaret Trimby

April 14 William s. of William & Mary Shepherd, of Zeals

April 27 Jane d. of William & Margaret Green

Aug. 1 Ann d. of Sam¹ & Mary Arnold, of Zeals

Aug. 25 George & James (Twins) s. of Rob¹ & Sarah Jupe

Sep. 1 Sarah d. of John & Esther Miles

Sep. 29 John s. of William & Mary Miles

Sep. 29 Silas s. of James & Susanna Bracher

Oct. 2 Dorothy d. of Rob¹ & Mary Miles

Dec. 8 Thomas s. of John & Hannah Feltham

Dec. 10 George s. of James & Mary Baker

Dec. 15 Susanna d. of John & Hannah Top

1772.

Jan. 5 William s. of James & Mariam Curtis

Feb. 23 Hannah d. of Sam¹ & Ann Edwards

April 11 Thomas s. of Thomas & Mary Lampard

April 20 George s. of William & Margaret Green

April 26 Thomas s. of Philip & Ann Miles

May 10 Sarah d. of John & Margaret Baker, bapt⁴ at Kilmington Ch.

June 21 George s. of James & Ann Meaden, of South Brewham

Aug. 2 Jane d. of John & Mary Rial

Aug. 23 Thomas s. of John & Betty Markey

Oct. 18 Melliar d. of Rob¹ & Ann Lapham

Nov. 15 Ann d. of Rich⁴ & Mary Clements

Dec. 20 John s. of William & Mary Baker

1773.

Jan. 17 George s. of William & Unity Rutley, of Zeals

Jan. 31 John s. of Rob¹ & Mary Howey

Feb. 11 Richard s. of John & Mary Bradden

Feb. 28 Susanna d. of John & Hannah Feltham

Mar. 21 James s. of John & Ann Jupe

Mar. 21 Israel s. of James & Mary Jillet

Mar. 24 John s. of William & Mary Feltham

April 4 John s. of John & Ann Evil

May 30 Lizzie d. of John & Ruth Bishop

June 13 Ann d. of James & Sarah Whitaker

June 20 Aun d. of Thomas & Ann Charlton

July 13 Hannah d. of James & Ann Arnold

Aug. 23 Maria d. of Samuel & Phaniah Gover

Sep. 23 Frances Alicia d. of Felix & Alicia Faugoin

Sep. 26 Josias s. of John & Margaret Trimby

Oct. 10 Thomas s. of Will™ & Rachel Bishop, of Kilmington

Oct. 13 Mary d. of Joseph & Grace Elmes

Nov. 28 Thomas s. of John & Betty Markey

1774.

Jan. 16 Ann Edwards illegitimate d. of Sarah Lapham

Jan. 23 Charles s. of Rob¹ & Sarah Jupe

Feb. 13 James s. of Richard & Mary Clements, born Feb. 6*

Feb. 20 Thomas s. of James & Ann Edwards

Feb. 27 Ann Edwards illegitimate d. of Mary Yetman

Mar. 6 Sarah d. of Samuel & Susanna Swetman

Mar. 20 Edward s. of James & Susanna Bracher

April 10 Edward s. of Thomas & Mary Lampard

April 17 Jane d. of James & Mary Baker

May 1 William s. of Joseph & Hannah Burges

May 15 Hannah d. of William & Mary Baker

* Interlined.

June 12 Martha illegitimate d. of Elizabeth Meaden
July 3 Henry s. of Henry & Betty Miles
July 10 Martha d. of John & Mary Bradden
July 31 William s. of William & Unity Rutley, of Zeals
July 31 Sarah d. of Rich^d & Mary Coward
Sep. 6 Samuel s. of Edwd & Sarah Card
Dec. 4 Thomas s. of William & Ann Target

1775.

Jan. 15 Elizabeth d. of James & Mariam Curtis
Feb. 13 Joseph s. of Philip & Ann Miles
Mar. 12 Thomas s. of John & Elizabeth Chandler
April 9 Celia d. of John & Margaret Baker
April 30 Elizabeth d. of John & Hannah Topp
May 21 Mary d. of Thomas & Susanna Bracher
June 4 Robert s. of John & Hannah Feltham
June 4 Ann d. of Thomas & Elizabeth Tabor
June 6 Harriot d. of Felix & Alicia Faugoin
June 11 James s. of William & Sarah Philips
June 18 Sarah d. of William & Margaret Green
July 2 James s. of Thomas & Ann Charlton
July 16 Susanna d. of Matth^w & Mary Coobes
Sep. 24 Giles s. of Robert & Sarah Jupe
Oct. 7 John s. of John & Mary Norris (privately)
Dec. 25 Hannah d. of James & Ann Edwards
Dec. 31 John s. of John & Elizabeth Markey, of Zeals

1776.

Mar. 10 Betty d. of Rich^d & Mary Clements
Mar. 11 John s. of Sylvester & Elizabeth Goff, of Penn
April 8 Sarah d. of James & Susanna Bracher
April 28 John s. of John & Ann Jupe

July 7 Martha d. of Thomas & Elizabeth Tabor
Aug. 18 Joanna d. of Robert & Ann Tabor
Sep. 1 Thomas s. of William & Mary Feltham
Sep. 8 Thomas s. of John & Mary Trimby
Sep. 29 Elizabeth illegitimate d. of Elizabeth Rial
Nov. 17 Sarah d. of James & Ann Arnold
Dec. 25 Rhoda d. of Saml & Phania Gover
Dec. 27 Mary d. of John & Mary Bradden
Dec. 29 Anne d. of Henry & Elizabeth Miles

1777.

Jan. 5 George s. of Christopher & Hannah Norris
Jan. 5 Jenny d. of William & Unity Rutley, of Zeals
Mar. 26 Amelia illegitimate d. of Margaret Edwards
April 20 Sarah d. of Felix & Alicia Faugoin
May 25 Joseph s. of Thomas & Ann Charlton
June 19 Charles s. of Thomas & Elizabeth Smart
June 23 Thomas s. of Joseph & Hannah Burgis
July 6 Catherine d. of William & Ann Evile
July 20 James s. of Rich^d & Mary Coward
Aug. 24 William s. of Abraham & Jane Morse
Aug. 31 Martha d. of John & Hannah Feltham
Oct. 5 Harriot d. of Uriah & Sarah Edwards
Nov. 11 William s. of Edward & Sarah Card
Nov. 18 Richard s. of William & Joyce Chafing
Nov. 23 Elizabeth d. of Rich^d & Jane Wood
Nov. 23 Matthew s. of Rich^d & Mary Clements
Dec. 14 Charlotte d. of Joseph & Grace Elmes

1778.

Jan. 11 William s. of John & Elizabeth Markey

Feb. 1 Eli s. of John & Margaret Baker

April 5 Elizabeth d. of Edward & Mary Goddard, of Bayford

May 10 Sophia d. of Thomas & Elizabeth Smart

May 17 Jacob s. of Robert & Sarah Jupe

July 12 Sarah illegitimate d. of Mary Yeatman

July 12 George s. of John & Elizabeth Hole, of South Brewham

July 19 Harriot d. of John & Mary Marshall

Aug. 23 William s. of John & Grace Child

Sep. 20 William s. of John & Hannah Lapham

Sep. 20 Ann d. of William & Unity Rutley, of Zeals

Dec. 25 Joseph s. of John & Hannah Feltham, p. b.

Dec. 26 Mary d. of Abraham & Jane Morse

Dec. 26 Mary d. of Felix & Elizabeth Lampard, of Mere

Dec. 28 Elizabeth d. of Robert & Ann Tabor

1779.

Mar. 14 Thomas s. of James & Miriam Curtis

Mar. 14 Mary d. of Philip & Ann Miles

April 5 Emmanuel s. of John & Mary Trimby

May 23 James s. of Charles & Rachel Smith

May 23 Sarah d. of William & Mary Baker

May 30 Richard s. of John & Mary Bradden

June 6 William s. of Thomas & Elizabeth Tabor

June 6 Thomas s. of John & Ann Jupe

July 11 Hannah d. of William & Ann Evil

Aug. 22 Samuel s. of Uriah & Sarah Edwards

Oct. 10 Elizabeth d. of Richard & Mary Clement

Nov. 3 Elizabeth d. of William & Joyce Chafing

Nov. 29 Mary d. of Elias & Ann Green

Dec. 13 Matilda d. of Felix & Alicia Faugoin

Dec. 25 James s. of John & Mary Marshal

1780.

Jan. 9 Mary d. of John & Hannah Feltham

Mar. 5 Samuel s. of Edward & Elizabeth Edwards

Mar. 15 John s. of John & Mary Phillips, pr. b.

Mar. 19 Ann d. of Joseph & Martha Lapham

Mar. 31 Elizabeth d. of John & Elizabeth Markey

April 2 Esau s. of Robert & Sarah Jupe

April 13 Harriot d. of John & Margaret Baker

April 20 Sarah d. of Edward & Sarah Card

April 23 Biatus s. of Sam¹ & Phaniah Gover

May 6 Sarah d. of John & Grace Child

May 7 Thomas s. of Robert & Ann Tabor

May 14 Helen d. of Abrᵐ & Jane Morse

May 21 John s. of Thomas & Elizabeth Smart

July 10 Elizabeth d. of Henry & Mary Hurle

July 16 Richard s. of Henry & Betty Miles

July 26 Giles s. of Giles Forward, from Woolverton, Mere

Aug. 10 Thomas s. of Thomas & Mary Draper

Oct. 22 William s. of John & Mary Bradden

Dec. 13 Rachael d. of Daniel & Elizabeth Dowden, from Zeals

1781.

Jan. 19 Ann d. of John & Jemima Coffin

Feb. 25 William s. of Elias & Ann Green

Feb. 25 Mary d. of Stephen & Ann Maidment

Mar. 4 Mary & Sarah Twin ds. of James & Mary Baker

Mar. 18 Mary illegitimate d. of Eliz. Windsor

April 15 Charles s. of Charles & Rachael Smith

April 16 John s. of John & Betty Owen, alias Hartgill

May 13	Edith d. of Uriah & Sarah Edwards, from Boreton
June 4	John s. of Richard & Jane Wood
July 1	William s. of Char[s] & Esther Jeffries, from Zeals
July 1	Samuel s. of Tabitha Whitaker (illegitimate)
July 8	Lætitia d. of George & Mary Bracher
July 15	Edward illegitimate s. of Martha Edwards
July 29	Hannah d. of John & Mary Marshal
Aug. 3	Isachar s. of William & Keziah Collins
Aug. 12	Harriot d. of Richard & Mary Clement
Aug. 19	Mary d. of John & Mary Trimby
Sep. 23	James s. of Philip & Ann Miles
Oct. 21	Betty d. of Joseph & Martha Lapham
Nov. 4	James s. of James & Ann Clements, from Gillingham, p. b.
Nov. 16	James s. of Edward & Elizabeth Edwards
Nov. 18	Mary d. of William & Mary Feltham
Nov. 25	Henry s. of Thomas & Elizabeth Tabor

1782.

Jan. 19	Elizabeth d. of Benjamin & Mary Bishop
Jan. 20	Maria d. of John & Hannah Lapham
Jan. 27	Carolina d. of James & Mary Mullins, of Zeals
Feb. 3	John s. of William & Mary Baker
Feb. 10	Frances d. of John & Grace Child
Feb. 17	James s. of John & Elizabeth Markey
Feb. 17	Marianne d. of Charles & Dianah Gover
Mar. 3	Ann d. of John & Mary Green
Mar. 31	Catherine d. of William & Ann Evil
April 23	Jane d. of Felix & Alicia Faugoin
April 28	Robert s. of Thomas & Elizabeth Smart
April 28	John s. of Thomas & Mary Draper

June 16	Susannah d. of Henry & Mary Hurle
June 23	Robert s. of John & Ann Jupe
July 7	Edmund s. of John & Margaret Baker
July 28	Ann d. of James & Sarah Mellish
Aug. 25	Harriot d. of John & Esther Miles
Sep. 15	Edward s. of Edward & Sarah Card (pr. b.)
Oct. 15	Hannah d. of Joseph & Martha Lapham, p. b.
Oct. 20	Elizabeth d. of John & Betty Owen, al[s] Hartgill
Dec. 1	James s. of Robert & Ann Tabor
Dec. 1	Betty d. of Henry & Betty Miles
Dec. 22	Charles s. of Charles & Diana Gover
Dec. 26	John illegitimate s. of Ann Rial
Dec. 26	Sarah d. of John & Mary Marshal

1783.

Jan. 12	John s. of John & Sarah Harcourt
Feb. 9	Martha d. of George & Mary Bracher
April 10	Ketura d. of Uriah & Sarah Edwards, from Bourton, p. b.
May 11	Sarah d. of Elias & Ann Green
May 18	Elizabeth d. of John & Mary Phillips
Aug. 24	John s. of Richard & Mary Clement
Aug. 24	Henry Upward illegitimate s. of Martha Target
Sep. 30	Catherine & Susannah ds. of Richard & Jane Wood, p. b.

Tax for Registring commenced Oct. 2.

Oct. 19	Sarah d. of Matthew & Elizabeth Gant
Nov. 16	Harriot d. of William & Keziah Collins
Dec. 7	Sarah illegitimate d. of Teresa Edwards
Dec. 26	William s. of Charles & Rachael Smith
Dec. 28	Susanna d. of Edward & Elizabeth Edwards

G

1784.

Jan. 18 Joseph s. of John & Elizabeth Markey
Feb. 25 Elizabeth d. of John & Mary Green
April 10 John s. of John & Grace Child
June 6 Mary illegitimate d. of Frances Walter
July 11 Jane d. of John & Mary Marshal
July 25 Mary d. of Edward & Ann Hiscock
Aug. 8 Joshua s. of John & Hannah Lapham
Aug. 27 Maachab & Hulda Twin ds. of Samuel & Phaniah Gover
Oct. 17 Charles s. of John & Mary Bradden
Oct. 17 Ann d. of Matthew & Elizabeth Gant
Nov. 5 Anna Maria d. of Felix & Alicia Faugoin
Dec. 12 Immanuel s. of John & Margaret Baker
Dec. 26 Albin s. of William & Mary Feltham

1785.

Jan. 5 Sarah d. of John & Mary Norris
Feb. 2 Elizabeth d. of Henry & Mary Hurle
Feb. 13 Phaniah d. of Thomas & Ann Sandal
Feb. 20 Sarah d. of Thomas & Mary Draper
Feb. 20 Valentine s. of John & Sarah Harcourt
Feb. 27 Sarah d. of William & Hannah Evil
Mar. 27 John s. of Robert & Ann Tabor
Mar. 28 Sarah d. of Thomas & Elizabeth Tabor
Mar. 28 Thomas s. of Thomas & Elizabeth Smart
April 18 Phaniah d. of Uriah & Sarah Edwards, of Bourton
April 21 Ann d. of Edward & Sarah Card, pr. bap.
June 7 Harriot d. of John & Martha Trimby
July 10 William s. of John & Mary Stephens
July 14 Mary d. of Robert & Ann Davis, pr. bap.
July 31 Sarah d. of John & Ann Jupe
Aug. 21 Richard s. of Mr Richard Colt & Mrs Hester Hoare

Aug. 21 Charles s. of John & Mary Marshal
Aug. 21 Ann d. of William & Hannah* Evil
Aug. 28 Sarah d. of Richd & Mary Clement
Aug. 29 Hannah d. of Thomas & Mary Lapham, p. b.
Sep. 18 Timon s. of John & Susanna Farthing
Oct. 23 Ann d. of Richard & Susanna Charlton, of Zeals
Nov. 21 Fannetta d. of George & Mary Bracher
Nov. 29 William s. of Henry & Ann Lapham
Dec. 11 Joseph s. of Henry & Betty Miles
Dec. 12 William s. of William & Ann Arnold, of Zeals

1786.

Jan. 23 Ann illegitimate d. of Hannah Miles
Feb. 26 James s. of Elias & Ann Green
Feb. 26 John s. of Charles & Rachel Smith
April 10 Ann d. of William & Mary Baker, p. b.
April 27 Elizabeth d. of John & Grace Child
May 8 Elizabeth d. of Nathaniel & Teresa Blewis, p. b.
May 14 Hannah d. of Ezekiel & Betty Charlton, of Zeals
June 6 Mary d. of William & Sarah Stephens, of Kilmington
Aug. 6 Sarah d. of John & Ann Wakeford, of Frome Selwood
Aug. 11 William s. of William & Keziah Collins, p. b.
Aug. 13 Philip s. of John & Elizabeth Markey
Oct. 3 Emma d. of Silas & Emma Cox
Oct. 3 John s. of Henry & Mary Hurle
Nov. 26 Nanny d. of Thomas & Mary Lapham
Dec. 10 Ann d. of William & Ann Arnold, of Zeals
Dec. 24 William s. of John & Martha Trimby

1787.

Jan. 11 George s. of Richard & Jane Wood

* *Mary* written first and struck out.

Jan. 30   Mary d. of Joseph & Ann Maidment, p. b.

Feb. 11   William s. of Samuel & Sarah Rolles

Mar. 6   Harriet reputed d. of Charlotte Edwards

Mar. 6   Richard s. of Robert & Ann Tabor

Mar. 18   Elizabeth d. of John & Mary Marshal

April 9   Charlotte d. of John & Margaret Baker

April 10   Charlotte d. of Jonathan & Sarah Carter, of Zeals

April 15   William s. of John & Ann Lewis, of Bourton

May 23   Mary d. of John & Mary Green, p. b.

May 23   John s. of Richard & Mary Clements

June 10   Joseph s. of Matthew & Elizabeth Gaut

June 26   Pamela d. of Uriah & Sarah Edwards, from Bourton

June 29   John s. of John & Mary Hoddinot, as reported of Sherborne

July 1   Ann d. of James & Elizabeth Whitaker

July 8   John s. of John & Mary Stephens

July 15   John s. of John & Ann Bradden

July 22   Ann d. of William & Hannah Evil

Aug. 9   James illegitimate s. of Dorothy Ryal, of Kilmington, p. b.

Aug. 19   Daniel s. of William & Mary Feltham

Aug. 19   Sarah d. of Charles & Dinah Gover

Sep. 9   Elizabeth d. of Edward & Sarah Card, p. b.

Oct. 28   Harriot d. of John & Sarah Harcourt

1788.

Jan. 6   John s. of Giles & Frances Collins, of Zeals

Jan. 13   Leah d. of Ezekiel & Betty Charlton, of Zeals

Jan. 20   Sarah d. of John & Mary Philips

Feb. 17   Mary d. of John & Grace Owen

Mar. 9   Sarah-Upward illegitimate d. of Martha Target

Mar. 19   John s. of Edward & Betty Bratcher, from Zeals

Mar. 23   James s. of James & Mary Coward

April 9   Daniel s. of John & Elizabeth Markey

April 9   Martha d. of John & Mary Bradden

April 13   Thomas s. of Charles & Rachael Smith

April 27   Phania d. of Henry & Betty Miles

May 17   Elizabeth d. of Thomas & Mary Draper, p. b.

June 8   Richard s. of John & Hannah Lapham

July 15   Clarissa d. of George & Mary Bracher, p. b.

Aug. 12   William s. of William & Mary Baker, p. b.

Sep. 16   Mary Beasley d. of Felix & Alicia Faugoin

Oct. 5   John s. of John & Mary Carter, from Zeals

Oct. 11   John s. of William & Anne Smart, p. b.

Nov. 2   William s. of John & Susannah Farthing

Nov. 2   Mary d. of John & Grace Clerk, p. b.

Nov. 9   George s. of Elias & Ann Green

Nov. 30   Maria d. of James & Elizabeth Child

Nov. 30   Hannah d. of John & Anne Bird, from Zeals

Dec. 21   Richard s. of Richard & Mary Clements

Dec. 27   Rachael d. of William & Anne Arnold, from Zeals

1789.

Jan. 9   Anne d. of William & Mary Andrews, p. b.

Jan. 21   Elizabeth d. of Henry & Charlotte Upward, p. b.

Feb. 1   William s. of William & Hannah Evil, p. b.

Mar. 8   Elizabeth d. of John & Martha Combes

Mar. 20   George s. of Mary Bird, from Kilmington, p. b.

Mar. 29   Hannah d. of John & Sarah Harcourt

Mar. 29   Stephen s. of John & Ann Bradden

April 5   William s. of John & Mary Marshal

April 26 Betty illegitimate d. of Sarah Edwards

May 2 John s. of Robert & Ann Tabor. p. b.

June 1 Elijah s. of Uriah & Sarah Edwards, from Bourton

July 26 William s. of William & Ann Evil

Aug. 9 Harry illegitimate s. of Charlotte Edwards

Aug. 9 Rachel d. of William & Kezia Collins, from Zeals

Aug. 16 James s. of Matthew & Elizabeth Gant

Sep. 20 Charles s. of William & Joyce Chaffin

Sep. 20 Ann d. of Ezekiel & Betty Charlton, of Zeals

Sep. 26 Susannah d. of John & Mary Bradden

Dec. 13 Mary-Ann d. of Henry & Mary Hurle

1790.

Jan. 3 Stephen s. of John & Grace Owen

Jan. 12 Francis s. of Silas & Emma Cox, p. b.

Jan. 17 Stephen s. of John & Mary Bradden

Jan. 31 Thomas s. of William & Unity Perfect, of Zeals

Mar. 13 John s. of John & Mary Trimby, Kilmington, p. b.

April 21 James s. of James & Eliz^th Francis

April 21 Ambrose s. of Ambrose & Mary Child

May 9 Robert s. of Silas & Ann Shepherd, from Bourton, p. b.

May 14 Elias s. of John & Mary Green, p. b.

May 22 Emma d. of Edward & Martha Mathews, from Pen, p. b.

May 23 Elizabeth d. of John & Anne Bradden

Aug. 22 Susannah d. of Henry & Betty Miles

Aug. 28 Thomas s. of Richard & Sarah Row, p. b.

Aug. 29 Stephen & John Twin sons of George & Mary Bracher

Sep. 5 John s. of John & Mary Stevens

Sep. 5 Emma d. of John & Sarah Charlton, from Zeals

Sep. 26 Martha illegitimate d. of Frances Walters

Nov. 10 Emanuel s. of John & Mary Marshal

Nov. 17 Joseph s. of John & Susannah Farthing

Nov. 17 Susannah d. of John & Betty Markey

Oct. 27 Frederic s. of John & Charlotte Edwards, from Bourton, p. b.

Nov. 3 Martha d. of John & Grace Child, p. b.

Dec. 17 John illegitimate s. of Edith Maidment, p. b.

Dec. 23 Charlotte d. of Henry & Charlotte Upward, p. b.

Dec. 25 Honor d. of Thomas & Susannah Bracher

1791.

Jan. 2 Thomas s. of Thomas & Mary Draper

Jan. 8 Thomas s. of John & Susannah Windsor, p. b.

Jan. 30 Sarah d. of Thomas & Martha Willis

Mar. 6 Charlotte d. of James & Elizabeth Child

Mar. 20 Sarah d. of James & Mary Miles

May 22 Jane d. of Stephen & Ann Bourton, p. b.

May 22 Mary d. of Charles & Rachel Smith

May 22 James s. of John & Sarah* Harcart

Aug. 8 Rosetta d. of Robert & Ann Tabor, p. b.

Aug. 8 Ann d. of Emma & Silas Cox

Aug. 21 Phania d. of William & Mary Andrews

Oct. 9 Lucy d. of John & Mary Philips

Oct. 1 Thomas s. of Richard & Sarah Rowe, p. b.

Dec. 4 George s. of James & Eliz^th Frances

Dec. 11 Richard s. of Richard & Jane Wood

1792.

Jan. 15 William s. of Richard & Mary Clements

Jan. 22 James s. of Matthew & Mary Gant

Jan. 22 Charlotte d. of John & Susannah Farthing

* *Mary* erased.

Feb. 1 Delatia d. of Willm & Ann Arnold, of Zeals, p. b.

Feb. 21 John s. of Martin & Sarah Bishop, p. b.

Feb. 26 John illegitimate s. of Elizabeth Keins

Mar. 13 Margaret d. of James & Mary Miles

Mar. 25 James s. of William & Hannah Evil

April 9 Jane d. of James & Ann Smart, of Bourton

April 9 James s. of John & Elizabeth Markey

April 28 Sarah d. of John & Martha Combs

July 8 Charlotte d. of Elias & Sarah Green

July 15 Benjamin s. of Ambrose & Rachael Cox

Aug. 12 James s. of James & Eliz^th Ryall, of Zeals

Aug. 15 Silas s. of Silas & Mary Shepherd, from Bourton, p. b.

Aug. 19 Abraham s. of William & Ann Smart

Sep. 2 Sarah d. of Charles & Elizabeth Jeffries

Sep. 13 Emma d. of Silas & Emma Cox

Sep. 20 Susannah d. of William & Keziah Collins, p. b.

Sep. 23 Thomas s. of William & Charlotte Crew

Oct. 14 Anna d. of John & Mary Green

Oct. 21 Joseph s. of John & Mary Marshal

Oct. 23 Robert-Montagu s. of the Revd Montagu & Caroline-Louisa Barton*

Nov. 4 John s. of John & Martha Hillier, p. b.

Nov. 18 Henry s. of John & Grace Child, p. b.

Nov. 21 Mary-Ann d. of Emanuel & Rebecca Matthews

Nov. 21 Robert-Horner s. of John & Elizabeth Charlton, p. b.

Dec. 25 Mary d. of John & Marina Doddrell

1793.

Feb. 9 George s. of James & Abigail Williams, p. b.

* Rev. Montagu Barton, Rector of Stourton, died 1790. This was a son of the Rector; he was Curate of the parish till 1796, and then Vicar of Broad Clyst till 1819.

Mar. 3 Thomas s. of James & Mary Moore, from the Lodge gate belonging to the Earl of Ilchester (extra parochial)

May 5 Thomas s. of John & Charlotte Edwards

May 6 Mary d. of William & Emma Webb, p. b.

May 6 Mary d. of William & Mary Baker, p. b.

May 19 Ann d. of John & Sarah Harcourt

June 23 Jane illegitimate d. of Edith Maidment

July 21 Mary illegitimate d. of Dinah Evil

Aug. 4 Sarah d. of Silas & Susannah Bracher, from Kilmington, p. b.

Aug. 18 Thomas s. of John & Anne Bradden

Aug. 29 Thomas s. of Abraham & Sarah Smart, p. b

Sep. 6 Alicia d. of James & Elizabeth Child, p. b.

Sep. 8 Mary d. of John & Mary Stevens

Sep. 22 Elizabeth d. of Martin & Sarah Bishop

Oct. 27 John s. of John & Mary Marshal

Dec. 15 James s. of John & Ann Bird, from Zeals or Bourton

Dec. 26 Hannah d. of James & Mary Miles

1794.

Jan. 14 Fanny d. of Immanuel & Rebecca Matthews, p. b.

Jan. 22 Charles-Pierson s. of John & Elizabeth Charlton, p. b.

Feb. 15 John s. of Richard & Sarah Rose, p. b.

April 20 Mary d. of Meshach & Fannia Hazard

May 5 Mary-Ann d. of Thomas & Mary Draper, p. b.

June 9 Sophia d. of George & Mary Bracher, p. b.

June 15 Sarah d. of John & Susannah Farthing

June 23 Abraham s. of James & Elizabeth Francis, p. b.

July 10 William s. of John & Marina Doddrell, p. b.

July 13 Mary (posthumous) d. of John & Sarah Harcourt, p. b.

Aug. 3   Charles s. of Willm & Hannah Evil

Aug. 7   Isaac s. of Willm & Ann Smart, p. b.

Aug. 17   Sarah d. of Matthew & Mary Gant

Aug. 31   Jane d. of William & Mary Grey

Aug. 31   Henry s. of the above William & Anne Grey, a former wife, admitted into the Church at the age of 7 years

Oct. 14   Thomas s. of William & Mary Target, p. b.

Oct. 26   Alicia d. of William & Mary Andrews

Nov. 9   George s. of John & Mary Marshal

Dec. 21   Betty d. of James & Elizabeth Welch

1795.

Jan. 11   Rachel d. of Ambrose & Rachel Coxe

Feb. 3   Sarah d. of John & Grace Child, p. b.

Feb. 4   John s. of Elias & Sarah Green, p. b.

Feb. 7   John s. of John & Charlotte Edwards, p. b.

Feb. 13   Fannia d. of James & Hannah Perfect, p. b.

Feb. 15   Sarah d. of John & Mary Green

Feb. 27   Eli s. of Martin & Sarah Bishop, p. b.

Mar. 1   Sophia d. of John & Anne Bird, from Zeals or Bourton

April 5   Hannah d. of James & Elizabeth Arnold

April 19   Edith d. of John & Elizabeth Charlton, p. b.

May 7   Honor d. of Daniel & Anne Meggs, from Bourton

May 22   Alfred s. of Robert & Ann Tabor, p. b.

June 7   Henry s. of John & Martha Hillier, p. b.

June 7   George s. of Charles & Rachel Smith

July 29   Amelia d. of William & Hannah Coxe, p. b.

Aug. 11   Keziah d. of William & Keziah Collins

Aug. 23   Susannah d. of Gabriel-Eli & Elizabeth Grenier

Aug. 23   Mary d. of James & Elizabeth Ryal

Aug. 24   Thomas & William twin sons of William & Ann Smart, p. b.

Sep. 27   Anne d. of Charles & Elizabeth Jeffries

Oct. 3   Betty d. of John & Sarah Hole, from Kilmington

1796.

Jan. 3   Mary d. of John & Mary Marshall

Jan. 10   William s. of George & Sarah Brodrip, p. b.

Feb. 28   Ann d. of John & Ann Bradden

Feb. 28   William s. of Meshach & Phauiah Hazard

Mar. 13   John s. of Thomas & Sarah Markey

April 17   William s. of Willm & Mary Target

May 15   Ann d. of John & Martha Felthem

May 29   Edmund s. of Matthew & Elizabeth Gaunt

June 12   Mary d. of Abraham & Sarah Smart

June 26   Martha d. of W^m & Amy Webb, p. b.; publickly baptized Sep. 9

Oct. 9   Joseph s. of Willm & Ann Smart

Oct. 30   George s. of Richard & Sarah Row

Nov. 6   Harriot d. of Mary Curtis

Dec. 25   Mary d. of John & Susanna Farthing

1797.

Jan. 8   Mary d. of James & Elith Welch

Jan. 17   Willm s. of John & Martha Helliar

Feb. 5   Ann d. of Charles & Sarah Tabor

Feb. 26   Willm s. of George & Mary Bracher

Mar. 5   Edmund s. of Jam^s & Elibth Arnold

Mar. 7   Amelia & Elibth ds. of Willm & Hannah Cox

April 2   Willm natural s. of Ann Bird

April 2   Mary d. of Jam^s & Elibth Ryall

April 23   Phaniah d. of Willm & Charlotte Crew

April 24 Ann d. of Jn⁰ & Charlotte Edwards

May 28 Philip s. of Ambrose & Rachell Cox

June 4 Will⁰ s. of James & Hannah Perfect

June 25 Will⁰ s. of James & Mary Miles

July 23 Betty d. of Will⁰ & Hannah Evil

July 30 Keziah d. of Will⁰ & Keziah Collins

Aug. 6 Robert s. of Robert & Martha Grey, of Mere

Aug. 6 Catharine d. of Jn⁰ & Ann Charlton (Zeals)

Sep. 20 Eliz^th d. of Jn⁰ & Eliz^th Charlton

Sep. 27 Catherine d. of Gabriel Eli & Eliz^th Grewer

Oct. 1 George s. of Meshach & Phaniah Hazard

Dec. 25 Edner d. of Jn⁰ & Marine Doddrell

Dec. 25 Cha⁰ s. of Dorothy Miles

1798.

Jan. 14 Ann d. of Susanna Felthem

Jan. 28 Josiah s. of Martin & Sarah Bishop

Mar. 25 Henry s. of Jn⁰ & Mary Marshall

April 5 Sarah d. of Absolem & Susanna Bracher

April 16 Henry s. of Jn⁰ & Martha Felthem

May 27 George s. of Will⁰ & Ann Smart

July 22 Sarah d. of Ju⁰ & Mary Green

Sep. 23 Henry s. of Jn⁰ & Ann Bradden

Sep. 27 Joseph s. of Joseph & Iset Lush, Kilmington

Nov. 28 Will⁰ s. of Ju⁰ & Charlotte Edwards

Dec. 2 Will⁰ s. of Matthew & Eliz^th Gaunt

Dec. 25 Eliz^th d. of Jn⁰ & Susanna Farthing

1799.

Jan. 8 Ann d. of Stephen & Harriott Theobold

Jan. 13 James s. of James & Eliz^th Welch

Jan. 24 Robt s. of Will⁰ & Hannah Cox

Jan. 27 Eli s. of Isachar & Eliz^th Farthing

Feb. 10 James s. of Charles & Sarah Tabor

Feb. 24 Sarah d. of Will⁰ & Ann Smart

Mar. 10 Tho⁰ s. of Tho⁰ & Martha Higgins

Mar. 25 Eliz^th d. of Jn⁰ & Edith Norris

Mar. 25 Phaniah d. of Sarah Cox, Bourton

April 21 Charles s. of Absolem & Susanna Bracher

April 28 Jn⁰ s. of James & Mary Miles

June 2 Tho⁰ s. of Henry & Mary Hill

June 9 Betsy d. of Jam⁰ & Betsy Green

July 15 Amy d. of Richard & Sarah Rowe

Aug. 11 Hester d. of Cha⁰ & Eliz^th Jefery

Sep. 15 Charles s. of Cha⁰ & Catherine Sparrow

Oct. 27 George s. of James & Eliz^th Arnold

Nov. 3 Ann d. of John & Mary Stevens

Dec. 25 Charlotte d. of James & Hannah Perfect

Dec. 28 Sally d. of Tho⁰ & Dorothy Goddard, Stoke Trust^r

1800.

Jan. 5 Ann d. of John & Charlotte Edwards

Jan. 26 Elizabeth d. of Tho⁰ & Sophia Curtis

Feb. 6 Mary-Ann d. of John & Martha Helliar

Feb. 13 James s. of Will⁰ & Mary Whitaker, Kilmington

Feb. 16 John s. of Robert & Judith Felthem

Feb. 23 John s. of Abigal Williams

Mar. 16 Robert s. of Joseph & Dorothy Davis

Mar. 30 Catherine d. of John & Eliz^th Markey

May 18 Mary d. of George & Sarah Broderip

June 8 Joseph s. of Henry & Mary Miles

June 15 W⁰ s. of James & Mary Moore, of Redlinge

June 22 Amos s. of Martin & Sarah Bishop

July 29 Sarah d. of Will⁰ & Ann Smart

Aug. 27   Harriott d. of Elias & Ann Green

Aug. 27   Sarah & Ann ds. of Jn⁰ & Betty Cooms

Aug. 27   Edward s. of Richard & Frances Alicia Frowd (Old Sarum)

Aug. 27   Edward s. of Thoˢ & Charlotte Draper

Nov. 9   George s. of Esau & Amelia Evil

Dec. 18   Emma d. of Willᵐ & Kezia Collins

A Register Booke of Weddings in the yeare of oʳ Lord God 1578.

1578.

Sep.	9	Humffrey Victor & Katherine Rogers
Sep.	24	John Juppe & Edith Norris
Nov.	27	John Rogers & Margarett Astwicke
Nov.	27	John Estman & Juhan Cowles
Feb.	1	John Will'ms & Edith Chamberlan

1579.

Nov.	28	Edward Sandell & Grace Blacker

1580.

July	24	John Dean & Margarett [blank]
Aug.	28	Peter Petney & Alice Carter

1581.

" None were maried."

1582.

April	16	Will'm Toby & Juhan Porter
June	5	John Cawpin & Juhan Deye
June	25	John Kingman & Anne Ryoll
Jan.	27	John Cawpin & Avis Barber

1583.

" None were maried in yᵗ yeare."

1584.

April	21	Robert Shorte & Juhan Baker
Nov.	19	Thomas Rodwaye & Mawd Harden
Nov.	26	Henry Orpit & Ane Paratt
Nov.	26	Thomas Browne & Margarett Bonde
Jan.	28	Walter Spindleton & Elline Adams

1585 & 1586.

" I find none sett in."

1587.

June	26	Will'm Adams & Juhan Barome
Jan.	31	George Hilgrove & Annes Aburrowe

1588.

April	11	Steven Jacob & Juhan Worome
June	23	John Welch & Dorithe Bonde
June	30	John Beaken & Marye Greene
July	1	Will'm Rolfe & Dorithe Webbe
Jan.	18	Richard Peny & [blank] Kenbery
Jan.	13	Will'm Rose & Agnes Burt
Feb.	1	Fraunces Sandell & Edith Jenins

1589.

Mar.	31	George Spender & Juhan Jenins
Jan.	21	John Dean & Elizabeth Petney
May	4	Will'm Style & Juhan Sandell
Oct.	26	Symon Whale & Edith Rioll
Oct.	28	Richard Butler & Elizabeth Midwinter
Oct.	28	John Cornishe & Elizabeth Mealmonth
Nov.	3	Henry Tricenino (?) & Edyth Adams

1590, 1591, & 1592.

" I find none put in."

1593.

May	14	John Sandell & Julian Rioll
June	27	Charles Chaundler & Tomsen Bradden
Nov.	19	Will'm Barnes & Elinor Stylo
Jan.	20	Philippe Mannssell & Fraunces Cawpin

1594.

April	15	Edward Sandell & Margarett Bisshe
Sep.	12	Leonard Sandell & Elizabeth Barber
Oct.	20	John Phillipe & Juhan Mayes
Jan.	27	John Rioll & Mawd Stylo

1595.

May	18	Robert Davie & Juhan Snowcke
Nov.	10	John Elis & Annes Cuffe

11

1596.

Oct. 4	Edward Lawrence & Katherine Browne
Jan. 31	Will'm Blanford & Nem* Rioll

1597.

April 4	Richard Sanger & Annes Sandell
Jan. 23	Will'm Gibbins & Welthian Kinge

1598.

Oct. 8	Richard Mylborne & Julian Read
Nov. 13	Thomas Psons & Mary Kenison

1599.

Dec. 2	Charles Paratt & Juhan Brittain
Mar. 11	John Balch & Frannces Juppe

1600.

Jan. 19	Valentine Stile & Al*se Fleet
Feb. 8	John Bowden & Edeth Sandel

1602.

Jan. 14	John Borrow & Anne Belcher†
May 10	Roger Hardin & Dorithie Hull

1603.

May 16	Robert Ryall & Elizabeth Sandle
May 18	Thomas Kinge & Elizabeth Davis
Oct. 10	John Stacye & Katheryn Kyngssberie
Nov. 25	John Sandale & Grace Kyrbye
Jan. 9	Robert Sandle & Susan Barretter

1604.

Oct. 16	William Leaver & Jone Allen
Jan. 2	Thomas Ashford & Elizabeth Toby
Jan. 14	Francis Hilgrove & Elizabeth Lambe

1605.

Jan. 10	Richard Norman & Darrothy Kenniston
Jan. 28	Henry Bolster & Joane Hinton

1606.

July 28	William [blank] & Elenor Barnes
Nov. 26	John Lodwin & Mary Toby
Feb. 2	Thomas Cayford & Tomsen Lambe

1607.

Feb. 9	John Dindy & Alice Feltham
Sep. 19	William B.... & Jo.... ....
.... ..	.... & Alice ....*
Oct. 18	Thomas Bowne & Margaret Davis

1608.

Feb. 1	Walter Lodwin & Johane Butt
Sep. 9	John Dean & Frauncis Smith
Jan. 24	John Yeades & Jane Davis
Feb. 20	Robert Saundell & Agnis Stronge

1609.

Oct. 2†	Frauncis Bacon & Jane Punchinby
Oct. 16‡	Thomas Saundell & Anne Bacon

1610.

July 26	Frauncis Saundell & Elizabeth Saundell
July 30	John Garrett & Margarett Sheppard
Jan. 23	Robert Brittaine & Julian Milborne, widowe

1611.

May 27	Willia' Cuffe & Elizabeth King, widow
July 8	Tymothe Fleet & Cicelie Shepheard
Sep. 16	Robert Chanler & Dorathye Meslin
Oct. 28	John Batten & Joan Browne
Jan. 13	Henry Harvy & Alice Stile
Feb. 8	James Alford & Margret Giles

1612.

"No mariages."

1613.

April 19	John Dewe & Elizabeth Gilbert
Nov. 8	John Cuffe & Joan Hill

* Perhaps *Neni*.
† The same entry occurs in the Register of Baptisms under the year 1601, which is probably the correct date.

* In these two entries the ink is almost lost.
† *Sep.* 23 written first and struck out.
‡ *Nov.* 7 written first and struck out.

1614.

May 23 John Bradden & Joan Pickford
Aug. 15 John Cleves & Joan Batten
Sep. 19 Will'm Riall & Agnes Miles

1615.

Jan. 29 John Ryall & Elinor Milburne

1616.

Jan. 27 James Alford & Joane Toope

1617.

(?) 29 Laurence Role & Elinor Style

1618.

Oct. 12 John Pierce & Alice Watts

1619.

May 24 Thomas Tabor & Mary Greene
Dec. 14 Robert Sandall & Agnes Coward

1620.

Oct. 23 John Dauie & Elizabeth Sandell
Oct. 26 John Sandell & Dorithy Castle
Nov. 9 John Smart & Maude Ellis

1621.

April 9 Edward Winsore & Anne Haisom
April 30 Will'm Rodway & Lucie Sandall
Sep. 24 Thomas Starre & Susan Rose
Jan. 28 John White & Constance Brittain
Mar. 4 Edward Elliot & Cicely Northover

1622.

Nov. 25 Josias White alias Josse & Elizabeth Dauis
Nov. 27 John Bacon & Elizabeth Martine

1623.

April 21 Thomas Rede & Marie Harding
Nov. 15* Willia' Holldway & Solina Tobie

1625.

April 25† John Luckis & Joane Davis
Oct. 3 Edward Rodway & Susan Rolph‡
Nov. 24 Anthonie Newma' & Anne Sa'dle

* This entry is dated in D. R. Nov. 14, 1624.
† This entry is entered under 1623, and struck out, and rewritten in another hand here. In D. R. it is dated April 23, 1624.
‡ Interlined: omitted in D. R.

1626.

"Mariages none."

1627.

April 2 Thomas Preslie & Agnes Britaine
Nov. 3 Thomas Moore & Margaret Joup
Nov. 20 Dauid White & Christian Preslie

1628.

Nov. 29 Edward Sewt' & Julian Hilgrove
Feb. 3 Alexander Lawes & Anne Bernard

1629.

June 22 Thomas Perry & Margaret Davis

1630.

June 21 Robert Ryole & Joane Dowdin
Oct. 8 Robert Kenison & Anne Curtis
Feb. 7 John Moulton & Catherine Euelry

1631.

July 10 Robert Joupe & Anne Davis

1632.

May 14 John Kinge & Jane Edwards
Oct. 21 Walter Britaine & Edeth Denmead
Nov. 1 James Pese* & Joane Day

1633.

Sep. 23 William Abshalom & Joane Ryall
Nov. 11 Francis Joupe & Margaret Bernard

1634.

Oct. 13 John Sandle & Edith Mores
Oct. 30 Richard Cousins & Marie Brittaine
Jan. 15 William Joupe & Margaret Ellis

1635.

April 16 Philip Carpenter & Christian Brittaine
June 29 Walter Brittaine & Dorothie Shepheard
July 20 Robert Davis & Katherine Williams

* In D. R. Peace.

Oct. 12   Robert Sandle & Elizabeth Blanford

Oct. 12   Edward Pickford & Amie Farding

1636.

Nov. 3   Andrew Grimes & Maude Stile

1637.

Sep. 4   Robert Boarde & Hester Russe

1638.

April 19   Steuen Bradden & Anne Combes

June 11   John White & Edith Board

Oct. 4   Valentine Pitnic & Elenor Day

1639.

" Marriages none."

1640.

April 16   Thomas Stone & Marie Franke

April 20   Mathew Combes & Elizabeth Boarde

Mar. 4   William Still & Susanna Garret

1641.

Feb. 3   Nicholas Lawrence & Cicely Hinkstridge

1642.

Aug. 15   John Welch & Jane Sandle

1643.

Nov. 30   Richard Younge & Susan Brittaine

1644.

Jan. 30   Thomas Stile & Edith Gibson

1645.

June 2   Cutbert Trimboy & Agnes Windsor

Oct. 20   John Dauis & Joane Clecues

1646.

April 6   Mathew Dowland & Anne Toope

July 20   John Trimboy & Anne Open

1647, 1648, 1649, 1650, 1651, 1652.
" Marriages none."

1653.

July 18   William King & Elizabeth Forward

Sep. 8   Mr William Huish & Mrs Anne Gibbon

1658.

Aug. 30   Mr Edward Amy & Mrs Joane Adderly

Oct. 18   Richard Brixie & Elizabeth Collins

1661.

May 30   William Vining & Rebecca Russell

1663.

April 29   John Forward & Anne White

Jan. 14   John Carrier & Basill Dauis

Feb. 4   Robert Goden & Grace Baker

1664.

July 21   William Sandle & Elizabeth Wakefield

July 25   Roger Lewens & Elizabeth Dauis

July 28   Nicholas Perric & Anne Tucker

1665.

Mar. 8   Mr John Abiugton & Mrs Elizbeth Feild

1666.

Feb. 5   Robert Riall & Mari Coye

1667.

Oct. 20   Robert Tabor & Tomsen Sandall

1668.

June 2   Giles Pickford & Catherne Evell

Feb. 15   John Sheeppard & Joane Davis

1670.

May 14   Cudbert Garet & Mari Perri

Oct. 10   Ambrose Hill & Florence Hunte

1671.

" Noe marriages yt yeare."

1674.

April 20   Thomas Stone & Mary Ball*

April 22   William Evill & Mary Stone

July 12   William Brimson & Ann Baker

1675.

Oct. 28   Steeveu Bradden & Mary Foster

1676.

Feb. 24   William Guire & Susan Jeffery

* D. R. adds, of Tisbury.

1677.

"Noe marriages yᵗ yeare."

1678.

Nov. 28 James Strond & Martha Barnew

1680.

April 19 William Hill & Elizabeth Suter
Aug. 5 Frances Sweatman & Ann Jeuson
Oct. 31 John Monke & Mellior Joupe

1683.

June 10 John Rowles & Cicilly Willis
Oct. 10 John Heyter & Dorathy Combs

1684.

Aug. 26 Laurence Butt & Judith Combs
Oct. 26 James Stroud & Mary Edwards
Jan. 26 Edward Royall & Joice Charleton

1685.

April 20 James Coles, of Brewton, & Mrs Florance Randall, of yᵉ same
June 12 Richard Gane (?), of Sherbon, & Lucy Hewett, of Meere
Oct. ? John Bradden & Ann Russell
Oct. ? John Stroud & Jane Sweatman

1686.

Oct. 10 James Stroud & Sarah Horlde
Nov. 4 William Rowles & Mary Scott
Nov. 10 Robert Throke & Mary Bowne

1687.

July 3 Anthony Lewis & Elizabeth Withers
Aug. 11 William Lamber & Alce Meaden
Feb. 27 John Heyter & Sarah Hooper

1688.

June 20 Edward Cobb & Issabell Butt

1690.

Nov. 3 John Trimboy & Elizabeth Leversage

[The first Register book ends here, and the second book begins the Marriages in 1702, in the middle of a page. The D. R. supplies part of the deficiency.]

1694.

Mar. 29 Thomas Ryall & Mary Bradden

1695.

April 6 Thomas Ryall & Mary Braden
M. 7 Walter Reed & Mary Stone

1696.

Oct. 9 Paul Sandall & Mary Berkett
Dec. 29 Francis Baker & Ann Oliver

1698.

Dec. 19 William Joupe & Mary Gregory

1699.

July 21 John Jupe & Mary Whatly
Oct. 3 George Gilbert & Elizabeth Davidge
Nov. 30 Richard Gubbens & Joan Targett

1700.

April 14 Edward Ryall & Mary Brimson
April 22 John Davidge & Ann Gilbert

1701.

April 23 John Holly & Margaret Em
May 12 William Frip & Ann Sandall
June 26 William Meaden & Sarah Sheapard

1702.

April 13 Thomas Tabor & Joan Sparrow
April 30 Devenish Sheane & Elizabeth Bradden

1703.

Aug. 16 Steeven Swaine & Febey Garrett
Dec. 14 John White & Mary Garrett
Dec. 30 Nicholas Dows & Milthred Cornelius

1704.

April 24 James Sparrow & Mary Curtoise*

1705.

April 12 Jonathan Mullens & Rueth Meaden
July 29 David Barns & Joane Hart
Oct. 17 Alexander George & Susannah Tilly

1706.

May 20 Samuel Lamb & Ann Maidman
Oct. 15 Robert Owen & Luce Meadon

* D. R. gives also, without dates :
John Suter & Ann Simonds, banns published.
John Sheapard & Mary Brikell, without banns or lycens.

1708.

July 20 Paul Toogood & Martha Butcher

Nov. 7 William Gibbons & Jane Thomas

Jan. 3 Robert Alford & Eliz. Evile

Jan. 17 Joseph But & Lydia Fry

Feb. 21 John Green & Mary Shepherd

1710.

May 22 Stephen Bourton & Joan Duffit

Oct. 8 Thomas Charleton & Rachel Wild*

Dec. 26 Thomas Ridgley† & Eliz. Michel

1711.

April 16 John Braldon & Mary Target

April 17 Edward Markey & Grace Garret

Nov. 26 John Evile & Mary Marshman

1713.

June 29 Richard Feltham & Mary Ryal, wid.

Aug. 11 William Brimson & Eliz. Chapman, of Horningsham

Sep. 15 John Baker & Joan Segram, of Kilmanton

Oct. 5 John Smith, of Gillingham, & Eliz. Combs, of Marck

Dec. 1 John Markey, of East Pennard, & Rebecca Garret

Dec. 28 William West, of Mere, & Eliz. Martin

Feb. 9 William Martin, of Queen Camel, & Mary Evile

1714.

Mar. 28 William Coward, of Mere, & Mary Bealing, of Gillingham

June 6 John Deacons & Catharine Edwards

June 24 Richard Lapham & Jane Edwards

Dec. 18 John Richards & Margaret Shepherd

Feb. 24 John Batten & Jael Jupe

1715.

April 28 Charles Evile & Catharine Joup

May 5 Edward Edwards & Rachel Mulleus

May 23 Joseph Suter, of Silton, & Ann Gulliford, of Mere

* In D. R. Wield.   † In D. R. Rugely.

May 29 William Barnes, of Froome Zelwood, & Mary Bealing, of Mere

June 15 John Feltham & Ruth Brimson

Sep. 1 John Edwards & Mary Evile

Oct. 6 William Brickle & Ann Topp

1717.

April 29 Philip Davis, of Cheesegrove, & Ann Martin, of Buggley

May 12 William Markey & Mary Meaden

Aug. 5 William Sharp, of Deverel Longbridge, & Anne Howel

1718.

Mar. 31 Thomas Easton, of Mere, & Grace Cox, of Wanstrow

April 15 Thomas Kiddle, of Stoke Trister, & Mary Maidman

May 5 Benjamin Brimson, of Munkton Deveril, & Ann Howel

May 22 Robt Baker & Elizabeth Owen

Dec. 22 Henry Cradock & Dorothy Chiles, of Gillingham

1719.

Mar. 20 Robt Godden & Eliz. Masters, of North Cadbury

1720.

Aug. 14 John Cornish & Margaret Childs, of Gillingham

Sep. 29 John Hill & Mary Burden, of Mere

1721.

July 2 Abraham Lawrence, of Mere, & Eliz. Dunn

Oct. 9 John Stone, of Gillingham, & Ann Stickland, of Kilminton

Nov. 1 George Edwards & Elizabeth White

1722.

Mar. 25 William Foaks, of Mere, & Alice Highman, of Gillingham, widow

Feb. 21 Samuel Target & Alice White

1723.

Dec. 23 John Bracher & Joan Swetman

1724.

Sep. 30 Edmund Inuber, of Sherrington, & Eleoner Bull, of Warminster

Sep. 30	John Mervin, of Bartley, & Elizabeth Lambert, of Kingstone Deveril

1725.

April 10	Charles Evil & Dorothy Barnes, of Gillingham
Aug. 8	Richard Maidment & Quirina Shepherd, of Mere
Nov. 1	William Feltom & Edith Cook
Nov. 22	William Bratcher & Elizabeth Green

1726.

April 25	William Heytor, of Mere, & Elenor Owen
July 11	Edward Edwards, of Kilmington, & Basil White
Feb. 13	John Carpenter, of Horningsham, & Basil Smart

1727.

May 24	John Baker & Mary Sandle

1728.

Jan. 30	John Trowbridge, of East Knoyle, & Frances White
Feb. 17	Henery Cooper, of Kilmington, & Jane Wills

1729.

April 15	Henery Miles & Margaret Hillier

1730.

[blank]	William Bradshaw & Ann Jerret, of Brewham
July 2	Francis Jupe & Eleoner Edwards, of Kilmington
July 23	Richard Edwards & Mary Paps, of Mere

1731.

May 3	Jonas Brimson, of Kilmington, & Ann Jacob
Nov. 13	Samuel Trewick, of Warminster, & Elizabeth Coward, of Mere
Feb. 3	William Forward & Amy Clarke, of Mere
Feb. 22	Francis Hibditch, of MoreCritch-Hill, & Rose Cheveral, of Hindon

1732.

May 21	William Harding & Lydia Fryar, both of Mere

May 25	Valentine Urson *alias* Harcourt & Catharine Tice, both of Penzelwood
July 12	Andrew Glover & Sarah Moger, of Mere
Aug. 5	Mr John Hartgill, of Killmington, & Mrs Jane Slater, of Stourton
Nov. 14	Thomas Candic & Mary Reeks, both of Mere
Mar. 11	Alexander Shord, of Warminster, & Elizabeth Carpenter, of Horningsham

1733.

May 17	Walter Tite, of Penzelwood, & Ann Bratcher
Aug. 11	Richard Bratcher & Eleanor Card, of Maiden Bradley
Oct. 7	Edward Forward, of Mere, & Elizabeth Apsey, of Brewton
Jan. 5	Joseph Burleton, of Mere, & Mary Richards, of Witham Frary
Feb. 21	Thomas Taber & Mary Evil
Feb. 24	Thomas Carpenter, of Horningsham, & Thomazine Taber

1734.

June 25	Abraham Lawrence, of Mere, & Elizabeth Web
Sep. 16	Thomas Chislet & Susan Ittery, of Mere
Oct. 18	Michael Lapham, of Kilmington, & Ann Owen
Nov. 3	Benjamin Griffin & Jean Turner, widw, of Mere
Feb. 15	John Anthill & Joan Butt, of Mere

1735.

Aug. 5	Philip Garret, of Wincanton, & Elizabeth Ryal
Dec. 21	Joseph Holly *alias* Pin & Mary Archer
Feb. 1	William Brown & Jane Fleet, both of Mere
Mar. 6	James Sanger, of Mere, & Joan Lockier

1736.

May 30	John Norris & Frances Down, both of Mere
Oct. 11	Joseph Mitchell, of Cann, Dorset, Edge tool maker, & Hannah Coleman, of Maiden Bradley
Dec. 19	Richard Maidment, of Mere, & Grace Pike, of Gillingham

1737.

June 8   Mr Christopher Ludlow, of
          Warminster, & Mrs Catha-
          rine Lampard, of Stourton
Sep. 7   Thomas Ridgley & Elizabeth
          Helleker
Oct. 26   Stephen Bradden & Mary
          Crumb
Jan. 5   Edward Foord & Margaret
          Suter, wid^w, both of Mere
Jan. 7   Thomas Brimson, of Killming-
          ton, & Mary White

1738.

July 26   Joseph Perry & Elizabeth Cross,
          of Maiden Bradley
Sep. 26   Joseph Hopkins, of Costley, &
          Susanna Hurine
Oct. 14   John Laws & Hannah Jupe
Mar. 3   Richard Prattent, of Shipton
          Mallet, & Elizabeth Baily,
          of Maiden Bradley

1739.

June 13   Robert Helms & Betty Ally,
          both of Costley
June 14   James Markey & Elizabeth
          Taber
July 24   John Target & Sarah* Edwards

1740.

Oct. 9   James Chapman, of Rodden, &
          Melior Pickford, of Maiden
          Bradley
Oct. 12   Richard Hayward, of Milton,
          Wilts, & Susanna Parsons
Dec. 1   John Stafford, of Bratton, &
          Joanna Cornish, of Gill-
          ingham

1741.

Nov. 21   John Pool, of Philips-Norton,
          & Mary Syms, of Maiden
          Bradley, wid^w
Mar. 6   John Jenkins otherwise Dea-
          cons & Elizabeth Arnold

1742.

June 12   William Foord & Mary Lever-
          suet, both of Mere
Nov. 10   John Baker & Mary Charleton
Feb. 9   James Curtis, of Wherell,
          Hants, & Mary Williams,
          of Mere
Feb. 14   Joseph Jacob & Elizabeth
          Jacob, of Zeals

          * In D. R. Mary.

1743.

April 8   John Sly, of Gillingham, &
          Ann Coward, of Mere
April 30 Robert Wier, of the Burrough
          of Hindon, & Eleanor Lovel,
          of Batcomb
May 28   Joseph Turner & Rachel Smith
June 27   Thomas Butler & Sarah Smith,
          both of Mere
June 27   James Shean & Sarah Ricks,*
          both of Mere
Sep. 26   John King, of Warminster, &
          Mary Folks, of Maiden
          Bradley
Oct. 4   John Evil & Mary Edwards
Nov. 26   John Street, of Mere, & Ann
          Suter, wid^w
Dec. 3   John Maidment, of Mere, &
          Sarah Burbidge, of West
          Knoyle
Jan. 10   Joseph Millerd & Joan Baker

1744.

Mar. 27   Henery Lewings & Love Har-
          vey
Mar. 31   William Gatehouse & Mary
          Read
June 13   Richard Charleton, of Mere, &
          Mary Busy, of Churton in
          Horsington
June 17   Silas Butler & Mary Barton,
          both of East Knoyle
June 22   Martin Moger & Elizabeth
          Butt, both of Mere
July 15   Robert Down & Mary Wil-
          liams
Aug. 14   Henery Miles & Elizabeth
          Owen
Aug. 14   Richard Matthews, of Shaftes-
          bury, & Jane Charleton, of
          Mere
Oct. 9   Morice Walter & Mary Feltom
Oct. 24   Thomas Ball, of Deverel Long-
          bridge, & Jane Broading, of
          Warminster
Dec. 26   James Sweetman, of Wincan-
          ton, & Betty Atkins
Dec. 28   Thomas Gould, of Longbridge
          Deveril, & Phebe Cox, of
          Kingstone Deveril
Jan. 8   Mr Nathaniel Still, of the city
          of Sarum, & Mrs Sarah
          Tatum, of Mere†
Feb. 25   John Down & Sarah Foord, of
          Mere

          * The name as first written has been erased.
          † Interlined.

1745.

April 1   John Ribb, of Mere, & Elizabeth Butt, of Gillingham

April 21   George Millard & Hannah Shepherd, both of Warminster

May 2   George Lapham & Ann Swain

June 8   Thomas Edwards, of Maiden Bradley, & Lydia Jacob, of Mere

Oct. ..   Anthony Hinton, of Longbridge Deverel, & Ann Brimson

Dec. 19   George Smith, of Mere, & Mary Thring

Dec. 28   James Sly & Mary Barnes, both of Gillingham

1746.

April 16   John Jupe & Dorothy Sandle

April 17   Mr John Butt, of Mere, & Elizabeth Lampard

Sep. 25   John Hill & Grace Hill

Oct. 20   James Sanger, of Mere, & Repentance Hockey, of Wincanton

Jan. 1   James Guire & Catharine Orchard

1747.

Aug. 4   John Perman, of Mere, & Margaret Chambers

Sep. 7   Joseph Stone & Mary Cook

Sep. 9   Samuel Sherrell, of Laterford in the parish of Houlton, Somerset, & Elizabeth March, wid^w, of Mere

Nov. 1   Thomas Lawrence & Elizabeth Deacons

Dec. 2   John Gauntlett, of Wilton, & Elizabeth Ware, of Keenton, Dorset

Jan. 1   Christopher Ingram, of little Knoyle, & Bettsy Thick, of Mere

Jan. 5   Philip Markey & Grace Kelloway, of Mere

1748.

April 21   John Rumsey, of Little Knoyle, & Ann Chisman, of Great Knoyle

April 26   James Nutt, of Froom, & Martha Elling, of Maiden Bradley

July 11   William Edwards & Martha Edwards

Jan. 3   William Shepherd, of Mere, & Catharine Hurden

1749.

Nov. 7   Thomas Knight, of Bratten, & Martha Owen

Nov. 30   Valentine Philips & Mary Boyt

Dec. 26   James Winslow & Betty Bond

Dec. 27   John Wadloe & Mary Edwards, wid^w

Feb. 20   Richard Coward, of Mere, & Ann Shepherd

Feb. 28   John Elling, of Mere, & Mary Hawkings, of Warminster

1750.

April 16   Joseph Lush & Margaret Coterel

June 14   Thomas Carter, of Zeals, & Ann Merrit

June 25   John Owen & Mary Miles

July 14   Richard Clement & Ann Ridewood

Sep. 20   James Sammells, of the city of Sarum, & Patience Witt, of Broad-Chalk

Nov. 15   William Markey, of Mere, & Mary Edwards

Jan. 16   Samuel Target, of Ambrosebury, & Elizabeth Lawrence

Jan. 29   Mr Gerrard Ellis, of Silton, & Mrs Ann Hill, of Stourton

1751.

July 13   George Green & Mary King

1752.

Feb. 21   James Harp, of Henley Harding, Warwickshire, & Ann James, of Mere

Sep. 18   Joseph Stone & Joan Edwards

1753.

May 11   The Right Honourable Charles, Lord Boyle, & Susanna Hoare, spinster

June 12   William Ellet, of Longbridge Deverel, & Hannah Owen

Dec. 26   William Tap, of Mells, Somerset, & Mary Bowles

1754.

Feb. 25   William Killoway, of Mere, & Ann Arnold

April 22   Stephen Stone & Jane Meaden

Sep. 9   Stephen Borten* & Hannah Philips

* D. R. Bourton.

I

1755.

April 9   Thomas Targett & Sarah Boyte

1756.

Feb. 7   William Smart & Sarah Bond
April 29   Thomas Evele, widower, & Mary Targett
Oct. 14   William Green & Margaret Sparrow, of Penn
Oct. 25   John Odbar, of Stower Provost, & Mary Lucas
Nov. 7   William Miles & Mary Rawlins,* of Kilmington

1757.

Jan. 20   Benjamin Ryall, of Kilmington, & Mary Whitaker; by licence
Aug. 10   James Lewton, of Kilmington, & Catherine Lapham
Sep. 5   George Arnold & Mary Wadlow
Nov. 12   James Dunn, of Gillingham, & Elisabeth Miles
Nov. 13   John Granger, of St Peter's, Shaston, & Elisabeth Burree

1758.

June 5   Stephen Stone, widower, & Martha Feltham
Aug. 13   Robert Green & Mary Odbar
Sep. 4   Francis Jerrard & Susannah Elmes, of Mere; by licence
Oct. 31   David Bratcher & Martha Bird, of Kilmington
Dec. 25   Robert Edwards & Grace Compton, of Kingston Deverell

1759.

Nov. 12   William Screen, of Penn Selwood, widower, & Ann Evill

1760.

April 6   William Read, a sojourner in this parish, & Martha Target
July 19   Robert Miles & Mary Hann
Sep. 30   Thomas Markey & Mary Stone; by licence
Dec. 2   John Owen, widower, & Lydia Papps
Dec. 25   Philip Miles & Ann Topp

1761.

April 21   William Shine, of South Brewham, & Ann Odbar

* In the register of Banns this is Lawrence.

July 11   William Edwards, widower, & Ann Owen, of Kilmington
Aug. 28   Edward Foord, of Mere, widower, & Sarah Spencer; by licence
Nov. 30   John Bracher & Sarah Leaver, of Berkley

1762.

April 26   John Rolles, of Kilmington, & Elizabeth Edwards
Oct. 10   John Eville, widower, & Ann Edwards, widow
Nov. 20   John Jefferies & Mary Edwards
Nov. 30   James Arnold & Ann Bracher

1763.

April 3   John Topp & Hannah Meaden
July 9   Robert Davis, widower, & Mary Holly
July 25   William Burfit,* of Silton, & Grace Owen
Aug. 28   John Baker & Margaret Trimby
Oct. 10   Thomas Holmes & Elizabeth Jupe

1764.

Jan. 17   John Talbot, of Wincanton,† & Betty Atkins
May 31   John Gover & Susanna Lapham
Dec. 2   William Feltham & Mary Edwards

1765.

May 5   William Target & Betty Jupe, of South Brewham
June 25   Mr Henry Hoare & Miss Mary Hoare; by licence
Aug. 25   John Mansfield, of Mere, widower, & Martha Edwards
Oct. 29   John Braddon & Mary Parker
Nov. 2   Thomas Trew & Patience Markey

1766.

Jan. 25   Thomas Shore, of South Brewham, widower, & Grace Burford, widow
Mar. 31   John Talbot & Ann Joy
April 1   John Jupe & Ann Baker
May 21   William Clement, of Merston-Bigot, widower, & Jane Goddin; by licence

* In the Banns, Burford.
† In the Banns, Charlton Hawthorn.

July	28	Samuel Odber & Mary Feltham
Aug.	31	Robert Smart, of Kilmington, & Basil Edwards
Oct.	12	John Albin Shore, of Whatley, & Elizabeth Heal; by licence

1767.

Feb.	15	Peter Gover & Christian Vining, of Wincanton
May	14	John Hurden & Rachel Atkins
May	22	Robert Howey & Mary Spinks, of Mere

1768.

April	4	Robert Moores & Mary Cross
April	5	John Miles & Esther Holly
May	26	James Turner & Hannah Edwards
May	30	James Davis & Priscilla Edwards
Sep.	26	John Bracher, widower, & Jane Tottershall, widow
Dec.	20	James Stacey, of Motcombe, & Sarah Gover
Dec.	25	James Baker & Mary Owen
Dec.	26	John Willis & Ann Bradden

1769.

Jan.	6	John Hacher, of Wincanton, widower, & Ann Tabor
June	16	Edward Markey & Elizabeth Kaines
Dec.	24	Joseph Bird & Jane Baker

1770.

May	7	Thomas Tabor & Elizabeth Bradden
May	20	Robert Lapham, of Kilmington, & Ann Edwards
May	28	John Read, of Cucklington, & Ann Chafey; by licence
June	25	John Shepherd & Ann Barnes

1771.

Mar.	31	Henry Miles & Betty Lapham
Mar.	31	John Feltham & Hannah Lapham
Mar.	31	Robert Jupe & Sarah Feltham
Oct.	8	Edward Kaines & Ann Feltham*
Oct.	20	Thomas Sandell & Ann Holley

1772.

| Jan. | 13 | Edward Bracher & Temperance Trimby |

* The Bonham Registers show that these were Roman Catholics.

Jan.	23	Thomas Bracher & Susanna Rose
April	28	James Shepherd & Mary Turner
May	25	Richard Clement & Mary Coombes
June	25	Peter Monamy Cornwall, of Tisbury, Clerk, & Mary Wyar; by licence
July	20	John Chandler & Elizabeth Granger, widow; by licence
Aug.	10	Thomas Talbot & Amelia Dunkerton; by licence
Dec.	25	Samuel Gover & Phaniah Baker

1773.

April	12	Samuel Swetman & Susanna Trimby
April	19	James Edwards & Ann Lawes
Oct.	3	George Lapham & Elizabeth Fallis
Dec.	19	Richard Coward & Mary Baker

1774.

Feb.	14	John Theobold, sojourner in this parish, & Ann March
April	3	John Smith, of Kilmington, & Betty Edwards
June	26	Matthew Coombes & Mary Jupe
Nov.	16	John Lapham & Ann Evill
Nov.	21	Charles Davis & Mary Barnes

1775.

Feb.	20	George Hill, of Gillingham, & Mary Moores
April	23	Robert Tabor & Ann Child
Oct.	10	Christopher Norris, of Monkton Deverill, & Hannah Lapham

1776.

| April | 7 | Robert Atkins & Joan Feltham |
| Oct. | 21 | Robert Dukes, a sojourner in this parish, & Mary Trimby |

1777.

Jan.	6	Uriah Edwards & Sarah Lapham
Jan.	25	Joseph Blake, of Bolder, Southampton, & Temperance Bracher, widow; by licence
Mar.	31	Jonathan Carter, of Mere, & Sarah Markey
April	6	William Evil & Ann Target; by licence
Oct.	27	Andrew Shepherd & Sarah Coombes
Oct.	30	James White, of Kilmington, & Sarah Moore; by licence

Nov. 17   John Child & Grace Portnall; by licence

Dec. 9   John Lewis, of Milborn Port, & Elizabeth Urry

1778.

Jan. 21   John Marshall & Mary Windsor

May 18   The Rev⁴ Mᶜ Salter, of Stratfieldsaye, Hants, & Delitia Barton; by licence

Aug. 10   John Odbar & Ann Shepherd*

Aug. 31   John Arnold & Sarah Frampton

1779.

Jan. 17   Charles Smith & Rachel Yetman

April 7   Henry Hurle & Mary Bowles

May 18   Edward Edwards & Elizabeth Curtis

Aug. 16   John Shears, of South Brewham, & Elizabeth Shepherd*

Aug. 23   David Boyte & Mary Sanger

Sep. 12   Joseph Lapham & Martha Trowbridge

Oct. 28   Elias Green & Ann Smart

1780.

Jan. 11   George Carter & Ann Odbar*

May 15   Joseph Howell, of Kilmington, & Mary Yetman

June 15   Stephen Maidment, of Mere, & Ann Feltham

July 20   Thomas Draper & Mary Target

Oct. 2   Richard Bracher & Mary Lapham, of Kilmington

Oct. 29   William Collins & Kezia Jupe

Nov. 12   John Collin & Jemima Matthews

Nov. 26   John Hartgill† & Betty Child

1781.

May 6   Matthew Gannt & Elizabeth Windsor

May 7   John Doddington‡ & Martha Hill

June 4   George Bracher & Mary Stone

Aug. 27   Alexis Green & Betty Coxe, of Pen Zellwood*

Oct. 7   John Green & Mary Edwards

Oct. 10   Benjamin Bishop & Mary Bond

1782.

Aug. 12   John Harcourt & Sarah Phillips

1783.

Mar. 2   Edward Hiscock & Ann Becket

May 1   John Jeanes, of Wincanton, & Mary Bracher

Oct. 12   John Trimby & Martha Edwards

Oct. 19   Stephen Bourton & Ann Alford

Dec. 5   James Horrell & Jane Snook

Dec. 25   William Moors, of Motcomb, & Mary Herridge; by licence

1784.

April 20   Robert Bird, of Kilmington, & Martha Stone*

Dec. 25   William Evil & Hannah Winsor

1785.

Jan. 19   Michael King & Mary Sparrow; by licence

Mar. 27   John Shuter, of Mere, & Catharine Topp; by licence

May 2   Thomas Lapham & Mary Bishop, of Kilmington

May 9   Joseph Lapham & Susanna Baker

July 4   John Farthing & Susanna Ryall

Aug. 29   Henry Lapham, of Kilmington, & Ann Baker

Sep. 13   Joseph Reffell & Susanna Taylor; by licence

Dec. 24   Richard Bracher, widower, & Mary Baker†

1786.

Feb. 20   Thomas Moger, of Shepton Montagu, & Frances Shepherd*

April 18   Samuel Rolles, of Kilmington, & Sarah Edwards

May 8   Joachim Odbar & Mary Bradden

Oct. 31   James Read & Charlotte Winsor

Nov. 5   James Whitaker & Elizabeth Combes

Dec. 24   John Owen & Grace Philips

1787.

Feb. 6   Charles Shepherd & Elizabeth Upward

April 10   Martin Bond, of South Stoke, & Sarah Love

May 1   David Short, of Wincanton, & Sarah Lewis; by licence

---

* The Bonham Registers shew that these were Roman Catholics.

† In the Banns, alias Owen : the signature is Hartgill.

‡ In the Banns, of Mere.

* The Bonham Registers shew that those were Roman Catholics.

† The Banns omit widower, and add widow.

May 21	Martin Odber & Margaret Shepherd*
Sep. 17	William Andrews & Mary Philips

1788.

June 20	William Williams, of Kilmington, & Quirina Maidment
July 15	William Rogis, of Gillingham, & Mary Bishop
Aug. 5	John Coombs & Martha Feltham

1789.

Feb. 23	John Bradden & Mary Markey
April 14	Ambrose Child & Mary Prankard
Aug. 24	John Philips, widower, & Mary Rolles
Oct. 25	William White, of North Brewham, & Elizabeth Freeman
Nov. 17	James Francis & Elizabeth Markey

1790.

April 5	William Shepherd, of Mere, but a sojourner in this parish, & Mary Matthews, widow
April 6	James Miles & Mary Evil
Sep. 29	William Markey & Jane Miles

1791.

Jan. 17	Emanuel Matthews, of Pen Zellwood, & Rebecca Pope
Feb. 20	Charles Jefferys & Elizabeth Lapham
May 2	William Crew, sojourner, & Charlotte Edwards
July 11	Thomas Charlton & Margaret Lawson,† of Shepton Montagu; by licence
Oct. 23	John Markey & Susannah Collins

1792.

Feb. 13	John Odber, widower, & Martha Davis*
Dec. 2	John Doddrell & Marina Miles

1793.

Jan. 15	Joseph Bird, of Kilmington, & Elizabeth Edwards
Feb. 5	James Williams & Abigail Phillips

* Roman Catholics.
† D. R. Leverson, but the signature is Lawson.

May 6	Thomas Mogg, of Upton Lovell, & Sarah Clark ; by licence
Aug. 12	Abraham Smart & Sarah Willis
Aug. 12	James Parfitt, a sojourner, & Hannah Miles

1794.

Feb. 22	Meshach Hazard, of Temple Coomb, & Fannia Phillips ; by licence
Sep. 14	James Arnold & Elizabeth Bishop
Sep. 23	George Brodrip & Sarah Bond
Oct. 12	John Markey & Elizabeth Parsons

1795.

Jan. 12	Richard Frowd, of Brixton Deverill, & Frances Alicia Faugoin
April 7	Charles Tabor & Sarah Miles
May 5	Thomas Markey & Sarah Davis
May 7	Joseph Lush, of Kilmington, & Isit Ryall ; by licence
June 6	The Honble Matthew Fortescue, of Filleigh, Devon, widower, & Henrietta Ann Acland, of Selworthy, Somerset, widow ; married at Stourhead, by special licence
Dec. 26	John Evil & Anne Edwards

1796.

Jan. 12	John Feltham & Martha Tabor
Feb. 9	Absalom Bracher & Hannah Lapham, of Kilmington
May 9	Anthony Moger, of Shepton Montague, & Marina Shepherd*
June 2	Thomas Goddard, of Stoke Truster, & Dorothy Ryall ; by licence

1797.

April 17	Henry Hill, of Mere, & Mary Bracher
April 24	Willm Smart & Ann Bird
Dec. 24	Henry Miles & Mary Sandell

1798.

April 9	Thomas Smart & Mary Edwards
June 8	Joseph Davis & Dorothy Miles

* Roman Catholics.

July 5   William Feltham, of Bourton,
          & Jane Target
Aug. 13   James Green, of Charlton Mus-
          grove, & Betsy Newton
Nov. 5   William Norris & Mary Hurd-
          ing, of Penzelwood
Nov. 28   John Norris & Edith Maidment
Dec. 26   Robert Felthem & Judith Ride-
          ward

1799.

Mar. 25   John   Markey & Elizabeth
          Bishop
Mar. 14   Thomas Pride, of Penzelwood,
          & Elizabeth Felthem ; by
          licence

June 6   John Ings, of Norton Ferris,
          Kilmington, & Susanna
          Hurle ; by licence
July 8   Richard Hatcher, of Marnhull,
          & Maria Shepherd
July 15   Charles Sparrow & Catharine
          Penny
Nov. 4   Thomas Curtis & Sophia Smart
Nov. 4   John Coombs & Betty Target
Nov. 25   William Markey & Ann Rutley
Dec. 26   Thom* Tabor & Eliz*h Markey

1800.

Jan. 9   Meshach Hazard & Ann Par-
          sous
July 27   Thomas Draper & Charlotte
          Crew

Buriall𝔰 in the yeare of oᵣ Lord God 1570 for yᵉ p'i𝔰he of Stowrton.

1570.

July	18	Christian Harden
Aug.	27	Leonard Davie
Oct.	29	Anne Botwell
Nov.	14	Juhan Borrowe
Nov.	18	Elizabeth Genigs*

1571.

Jan.	20	Christian Lambe
Feb.	20	Will'm Lamb the elder
Mar.	8	Will'm Sandell

1572.

June	4	Will'm Sandell
Jan.	30	Thomas Chawpin
Feb.	18	Richard Cowley

1573.

Aug.	22	Elizabeth Sandell
Aug.	24	Margarett Kenison
Jan.	21	Mawd Winter

1574.

Sep.	28	Dorithe Carter
Oct.	9	John Lambe
Nov.	24	Will'm Harte

1575.

June	5	Valentin Lambe
June	2	Annes Bone

1576.

Oct.	5	John Sutter
Mar.	16	Charles Kinge
Mar.	24	John Spender

1577.

May	7	John Rioll
July	6	Edward Aborrowe
Dec.	16	Richard Alford

1578.

Mar.	17	Elnor Hayne
June	2	Thomas Sandell
June	13	Moris Apresse
Aug.	29	Thomas Baylie
Sep.	5	George Rioll

* For *Jennings*.

1579.

April	3	Alice Baylie
June	15	John Genens
July	9	Christien Britten
Aug.	2	Annes Seath
Sep.	11	Margaret Wills
Nov.	8	John Davie

1580.

May	10	Richard Mychell
Oct.	25	Walter Kerwithe
Jan.	29	Walter Lambe
Mar.	17	Juhan Adams

1581.

April	22	John Stowrton, gent.
April	26	Alice Style
July	19	Juhan Davie
July	27	Marye Cooffe
Jan.	27	Robert Genens

1582.

Mar.	30	Juhan Robins
Oct.	13	Margerie Britten
Oct.	15	Juhan Cawpin
Dec.	14	Christian Sandell
Jan.	10	Thomas Pondford
Mar.	19	Valentine Carter

1583.

May	17	Mary Britten
June	21	Julian Geffery
Aug.	8	Edith Everard

1584.

May	27	Jane Byflet
Oct.	6	Eme Hill
Dec.	9	Fraunces Harden
Dec.	16	Robᵗ Whitchurch
Feb.	21	John Standwricke
Feb.	28	Margaret Mychell
Mar.	10	Alice Myller

1585.

May	28	Annes Davie
July	4	Jane Byflet
July	15	Walter Parret
Oct.	18	John Lambe
Nov.	4	Richard Blacker

Dec.   3   Elnor Bruer
Dec.   4   Robert Spencer
Jan.   1   Edyth Butler

1586.

May   6   Edyth Smart
May   28   Juhan Dean
Nov. 17   Juhan Hill
Nov. 21   Thomas Tooppe
Feb.   9   Gesper Smart
Feb. 14   Will'm Lodden
Mar. 19   Will'm Baylie

1587.

June   9   John Kingman
Oct. 11   Anne Rogers, gent.
Oct. 17   Ursusa Tayler
Oct. 20   Juhan Turner
Dec. 24   Juhan Hill
Jan.   7   Tomsen Britten
Jan. 29   Elizabeth Harden
Mar.   1   Tomsen Cha'berlene

1588.

Mar. 27   Elizabeth Kenison
April 15   Thomas Davie
April 19   John Blanford
April 19   Will'm Chamberlayne
April 22   Henry Barons
May   15   Juhan Spender
June 17   John Spender
July   6   Juhan Sandell
Nov.   7   Will'm Robins
Nov.   8   Juhan Davie
Nov. 25   The Right Honorable   Lord
           John Stourton*
Nov. 26   Margarett Brian, gent.

1589.

Feb. 19   Margaret Dean
Mar. 13   Elizabeth Sandell
Mar. 23   Margaret Tayler
Nov. 25   Jan Cawpin
Oct.   9   John Tooppe
Oct. 16   Samuell Lodden
Feb. 25   Edith Juppe
Oct. 22   Will'm Tooppe

1590 & 1591.

"I find none put in, & in the yeare 1592
I find but one."

Jan.   6   Edyth Chamberlayne

* This was the eighth Baron and the eldest son
of Charles, Lord Stourton, executed at Salisbury
in 1557 for the murder of the Hartgills. He was
restored in title and estates by Act of Parliament
in 1575.

1593.

April 27   John Davis
Aug.   1   Grace Sandell
Aug.   4   Will'm Morgan
Oct. 24   Will'm Britten
Nov. 29   Richard Adams
Feb. 15   Elizabeth Dean
Feb. 21   Will'm Hilgrove

1594.

April 3   Walter Davis
May   14   Annes Sandell
May   14   Annes Lawnder
May   25   Thomas Cuffe
Sep. 23   Annes Chamberlene
Feb.   4   Jane Davis
Feb. 10   Will'm Davis

1595.

Nov. 30   Christian Hutcheus al's Alen
Jan. 26   Annes Tayler
Jan. 29   Will'm Bruer

1596.

Aug.   1   Dorithe Hardinge
Aug.   3   Will'm Hardinge
Oct. 11   Peter Mathewe al's Flacher
Feb.   6   Margarett Adams
Feb.   8   John Cawpin

1597.

April 5   John Winter
April 15   Richard Kenison
April 28   Annes Tooppe
April 29   Sible Flacher
May   1   Giles James
July 15   Edward Blanford
Oct. 31   Leonard Rioll
Jan. 17   John Bonde
Feb. 23   Annes Rioll

1598.

April 30   John Juppe
June 13   Thomas Harding
June 24   Edith Blaufford
Oct. 29   Annes Standwricke
Dec.   2   Thomas Bennet
Dec.   7   Mary Parratt
Jan. 14   Will'm Mericke

1599.

Mar. 27   Jane Shard
Mar. 29   Maud Elis
April 29   Nathaniel Biles

[There is a leaf of the original Register
missing here.]

[1610.]

May 27 Mary Lodwin w. of John Lodwin
June 7 An Midwinter w. of Charles Midwinter
Oct. 10 Richard Milborne, Clerk* of Stourton
Nov. 27 Helen Davies d. of Robert Davies
Dec. 7 [blank] Lamb, widowe
Jan. 17 Hugh Burrowes s. of John Burrowes
Feb. 9 Christopher Davis, of Woodbridge

1611.

April 15 Agnis Jacob, servant unto Mr Stourton, of Bonham House†
April 16 William Kenison
April 18 Agnis Hilgrove w. of George Hilgrove
April 21 Valentine Stile
June 23 Charles Chanler
June 24 Avice Calpin, widow
Sep. 1 Mary d. of Walter Tabor
Jan. 9 Mary Munke, a stranger
Feb. 3 Owin Adams

1612.

April 5 James s. of James Auford
April 24 Ann d. of Alexander Greene
June 12 Thomas s. of John Sandall
Aug. 4 Margret d. of John Dean
Sep. 11 Peter Pitney
Sep. 11 A childe of Robert Barons, unbaptised
Nov. 16 Robert Davies, of Woodbridge
Nov. 18 Anne Daunt w. of John Daunt, gent.
Jan. 11 George Hilgrove
Feb. 12 Edith w. of Thomas Erbery

1613.

May 7 Margaret Kenison, widowe
June 26 Elizabeth w. of John Davie
Sep. 24 Francis s. of Francis Sandall
Oct. 11 Mary d. of John Parret
Oct. 30 Cicely Messalin, servant
Oct. 31 Catharine Blandford, widowe
Dec. 31 John Pitney s. of Peter Pitney
Jan. 31 Anne d. of John Dewe
Feb. 5 Alice w. of John Ryall

* I.e. Parish Clerk; there is a fresh nomination recorded on March 15, 1611.
† A stranger struck out, and the above interlined.

Feb. 9 Joan d. of John Ryall
Mar. 24 Henry s. of William Henkstridge

1614.

April 20 John Hill
Aug. 19 John s. of John Cuffe
Sep. 3 Elizabeth Ryall, widowe
Jan. 26 Tristram Gifford
Mar. 2 John Lamb

1615.

April 10 Joane d. of Robt Barnes
April 23 Tomason Chandler, wid.
May 25 John s. of Alexander Greene
June 9 Agnes Greene, wid.
Nov. 15 Joane w. of Willia Toope
Nov. 29 John Lodwin
Feb. 9 Susan Bleeke, wid.

1616.

April 10 John s. of James Alford
April 30 Reinold s. of John Joup
Dec. 12 Margarett w. of James Alford
Jan. 6 Catherine Gifford, vidua

1617.

June 16 Anne Davies, wid.
July 11 Mary d. of Thomas Board
July 30 Elizabeth Joup, wid.

[There is another leaf missing here, but the D. R. supplies part of the deficiency.]

1623.

Feb. 19* Robert Sandall
Feb. 22* Joan Encrad, widdow
April 5 John Perre
May 12 Walter s. of Walter Tabor
May 18 Robert s. of Doctor King
June 18 Joan d. of Robert Kinnison
June 22 Ann w. of Thomas Sandall
July 4 Joan d. of John Whitt
July 12 Roger Hill [or perhaps Still]
Aug. 21 Elizabeth Dean
Oct. 1 Edeth d. of Willi Brittain
Jan. 31 Elbeth Bacon
Feb. 12 Alice Petni, widdow

1624.

April 24 Richard s. of Richard Smith
Sep. 2 Robart Huchings
Feb. 26 Margeret d. of Walter Loddings
Mar. 16 Joane Sangier

* These two entries probably belong to 1622, but they are returned thus.

K

1625.

Oct.	8	Elizabeth d. of Docter King
Feb.	6	Henri s. of Roger Hulet, Curat
Feb.	6	John s. of John Cuf

1626.

May	4	Nicholas s. of Robert Barnes
June	23	Henrie s. of Henrie Edwards
July	11	Francis Deane
July	13	Juliane Stile
July	30	Constance Britaine
Oct.	4	Christiane Preslie
Oct.	6	Joane Irons
Oct.	27	Richard Britaine
Jan.	24	Anne Ellise

1628.

Mar.	26	Joane Lambe, widow
May	11	Willia' Baro'
May	17	Alice Davis w. of Charles Davis
Aug.	24	Agnes w. of John Borde
Dec.	24	Edbert s. of Edward Sewt'
Jan.	14	Thomas Sandle
Feb.	8	Winefrid w. of John Sandle
Mar.	12	Richard s. of Richard Smith

1629.

May	23	Edith Sandle
July	5	Elizabeth d. of Willia' Hinckstridge
Sep.	13	John Sandle
Sep.	24	Christopher Davis
Dec.	21	John s. of John Swetnam
Jan.	21	Anne w. of John Deane
Mar.	3	John s. of Richard Smith

1630.

May	23	John s. of Edward Sewter
June	7	Francis d. of Cutbert Trimby
July	19	John Vigars
July	19	Anne d. of Cutbert Trimby
Aug.	5	Edith Daye
Aug.	11	Emme w. of Willia' Blandford
Sep.	21	Tobie Daye
Oct.	13	Edith w. of Willia' Rose
Nov.	21	Agnes w. of Thomas Presly
Dec.	6	Jerom Parsons
Jan.	5	Margery Sandle, widowe
Jan.	26	Thomas Bernard, widow'
Jan.	28	Robert s. of John Sandle
Feb.	13	Joane w. of Alexander Davis
Mar.	6	John s. of Willia' Ryole
Mar.	7	George s. of George Baylie
Mar.	11	Urslie d. of Urslie Holdway

1631.

| July | 30 | Alice Harding, widow |
| Aug. | 8 | Mary w. of Leonard Sewt' |

1632.

May	3	John s. of John Cuffe
July	11	Lucie d. of Henry Edwards
July	22	Joane Dauis, widow
Oct.	20	Christopher Addams
Oct.	21	Edeth w. of Henrie Edwards, the elder
Feb.	19	Henry Barnes

1633.

May	8	M' Henry Clifton
May	25	The right Honourable Edward, Lord Stourton of Stourton*
June	24	Dorothie d. of Elizabeth Saudle
Aug.	10	William Bayly
Sep.	20	Martha Cotton, widdow
Dec.	1	Joane Parret, widdow
Dec.	3	Valentine s. of William Ryall

1634.

Jan.	4	Joane Shepheard, widdow
Jan.	12	Edith w. of Walter Brittaine
Feb.	4	Elizabeth Hillgrove, widdow
Feb.	8	Walter Hill
Feb.	11	Marie d. of Edward Shuter

1635.

April	21	Elizabeth d. of Henry Barnes
Sep.	20	Edward Sandle
Nov.	1	Edward Windsor
Nov.	29	Edith w. of John Joupe
Dec.	12	Walter s. of Robert Joupe
Dec.	16	M' Thomas Martin
Jan.	29	Charles Danis
Feb.	18	Thomasine Pitnie
Mar.	5	Alice w. of Edward Helier

1636.

May	5	Elenor w. of Valentine Pitnie
June	10	Leonard Snooke
June	18	Walter Tabor
July	20	John Combes
July	25	Marie d. of John Edwards
Nov.	21	William Ryall
Dec.	11	Agnes w. of William Ryall
Dec.	15	Dorothie w. of Walter Brittaine
Feb.	2	Joane w. of Walter Willis
Feb.	9	John Stile
Mar.	10	Joane d. of Edmund Ludlow

* The ninth Baron.

1637.

Mar.	29	Richard Cleeues
April	4	Edith w. of Richard Cleeues
May	9	Robert s. of William Blanford
June	11	Alice d. of Edward Shuter
June	13	Joane Taylour
Aug.	27	Cicely w. of Edward Elliot
Sep.	8	Nicholas s. of Robert Shepheard
Nov.	26	Marie w. of Thomas Reade
Feb.	26	John s. of John Sandle
Mar.	13	Marie d. of Gregorie Mouson

1638.

Mar.	30	John s. of Mr John Ewins
July	29	Margaret d. of John Prestly
Aug.	9	Joane d. of Edward Windsor
Aug.	15	Mathew Combes
Aug.	22	Julian Brittaine
Aug.	22	Anthonie Nueman
Aug.	27	Margaret Sandle, widdow
Aug.	28	William Brittaine
Aug.	28	William Rose
Sep.	2	Edward Elliot
Sep.	4	Joane Tabor, widdow
Sep.	6	James Combes
Sep.	14	Joane d. of William Holdway
Sep.	21	Alice d. of Humphry Lacy
Sep.	26	Anne Combes, widdow
Oct.	9	John Perrie
Oct.	18	John s. of John Sandle
Oct.	26	Jane d. of John Dauis
Dec.	14	Mary Sandle
Dec.	30	Elizabeth Day, widdow
Jan.	10	John Joupe
Jan.	11	Anne w. of Robert Kenison
Jan.	25	Peter s. of James Pesy
Feb.	23	Alexander Dauis
Mar.	13	Thomas s. of Thomas Walter

1639.

April	2	Robert Day
April	21	George s. of John Evill
May	2	Elizabeth Barnes, widdow
May	16	Joane w. of John Bradden
June	5	Edmund s. of Robert Toope
Aug.	5	John s. of James Pesy
Sep.	10	Joseph s. of William Poore
Nov.	30	Joseph Dauis
Mar.	22	Peter s. of Valentine Pitmie

1640.

June	19	Edith d. of John Sandle
July	25	Elizabeth d. of Lawrence Rowles
Nov.	8	Robert Garret
Jan.	25	William s. of Robert Joupe
Feb.	23	Henrie Edwards

Mar.	4	William Seymour
Mar.	9	Elenor Shropsheere

1641.

Mar.	31	John s. of Thomas Stone
July	27	Anne w. of William Toope
Aug.	5	Joane Lodwin, widdow
Dec.	6	John Bacon
Dec.	17	John Sandle
Mar.	5	Mr Francis Popely

1642.

April	16	Henrie s. of Eamme Ryall
July	15	James Allford
Nov.	14	Susan d. of Alexander Adams
Dec.	4	Maud d. of Lawrence Rowles
Dec.	8	Jane d. of John Welch
Mar.	5	Robert Kenison

1643.

May	25	Elizabeth Snooke, widdow
June	11	Jane w. of Nicholas Dier
Aug.	8	Francis Brittaine
Aug.	11	Margerie Rose, widdow
Aug.	31	Emme d. of Thomas Ryall
Sep.	5	Mathew s. of Mathew Combes
Oct.	25	Thomas s. of John Rodway
Oct.	26	Francis s. of John Rodway
Nov.	11	Thomasine w. of Thomas Ryall
Dec.	21	Mary Trimboy
Jan.	4	Francis s. of Doctor Chatin
Jan.	28	Alexander s. of Robert Dauis
Feb.	4	John Bradden

1644.

May	17	Thomas Prestlie
July	7	Joane d. of John Welch
July	13	Richard s. of Richard Younge
Aug.	12	Philip s. of Mr John Freake
Oct.	10	Anne Nueman, widdow
Oct.	11	John s. of John Euill
Oct.	19	Alice w. of Cutbert Trimboy
Nov.	20	Elizabeth Kenison, widdow
Dec.	22	George s. of George Greene
Jan.	5	Elizabeth w. of Francis Sandle
Jan.	15	John Dauis
Feb.	9	Robert Sandle
Mar.	10	Francis s. of Thomas Stone

1645.

April	15	Edward s. of Marie Sandle
June	10	Henrie Edwards
June	12	Christian Stile
Sep.	24	Winefride d. of William Inges
Oct.	26	John Sandle the Clerke
Nov.	29	Alexander Greene
Dec.	3	Katherine w. of John Bartlet

Mar. 11	Joane w. of Thomas Tabor
Mar. 24	Peter s. of William Poore

1646.

April 4	John s. of Edward Shuter
April 24	Katherine d. of John Legate
June 5	Richard s. of Rachel Chanell
July 26	William Stile
Aug. 2	William s. of William Pereman
Aug. 3	Margaret w. of John Board
Aug. 5	Mrs Francis d. of the right Honourable William, Lord Stourton
Aug. 20	Mr Robert Barnes
Oct. 6	Lawrence Rowles
Oct. 12	Widdow Bacon
Dec. 23	Richard s. of Thomas Hunt
Dec. 25	Elizabeth d. of Manuel Swetman
Feb. 22	Susanna d. of William Poore

1647.

June 24	Thomas s. of Robert Toope
July 4	John s. of John Rodway
Aug. 23	Marie d. of Richard Younge
Oct. 16	John s. of James Stroud
Nov. 17	Edith w. of John White
Nov. 28	Cutbert s. of Cutbert Willmot
Mar. 10	Anne d. of Margaret Combes

1648.

April 18	Martha Lunsdowne
Sep. 21	Thomasine Lodwin
Oct. 27	William Brickell
Jan. 18	Margaret Allford, widdow
Feb. 12	Thomas s. of Richard Younge
Feb. 23	Dorothie d. of William Inges

1649.

May 19	William s. of John Prestly
June 9	Mathew s. of Leonard Shuter
July 31	Agnes w. of Cutbert Trimboy
Sep. 19	Jone d. of Robert Ryall
Oct. 28	Elizabeth w. of Robert Sandle
Dec. 30	Margaret w. of Francis Joupe
Feb. 2	Richard Gibbes

1650.

April 5	William Blanford
April 5	Elizabeth d. of Richard Young
April 26	Anne Stile widdow of John Stile
May 17	Marie w. of Sir John Wild & d. of the right Honourable William, Lord Stourton
May 30	Joane d. of Robert Toope
May 31	Elizabeth Lambe
Aug. 8	Marie w. of Thomas Reade

Sep. 28	Jane d. of John Welch
Oct. 17	Joane Spender, widdow

1651.

April 16	Marie w. of Walter Board
July 16	John Swetnam
July 18	Manuel s. of Edmund Swetnam
Aug. 10	Samuel Sandle
Aug. 10	Susanna d. of William Poore
Feb. 20	William s. of Alexander Adams
Mar. 3	Susanna d. of Thomas Hunt

1652.

Mar. 30	Elizabeth w. of Robert Ryall
May 9	Edward Shuter
Aug. 5	Elizabeth Bradden, widdow
Aug. 19	William Bernard
Jan. 9	Sisely d. of John Rodway
Jan. 26	Leonard Shuter

1653.

May 28	Thomas s. of John Baker
June 2	Marie w. of Thomas Banister
July 6	Susanna Bayly
Sep. 12	Philip d.* of Philip Guppill
Oct. 24	Thomas Barnes
Jan. 8	Susanna Adams, widdow
Feb. 9	Alice w. of Robert Jaques
Mar. 24	Francis d. of Mr Charles Croke

1654.

Mar. 25	Anne d. of Thomas Wadly
Mar. 28	Marie d. of Edward Shuter
April 4	William Enill
April 4	John s. of Thomas Hunt
April 30	Elenor Sabbots
May 16	Dorothie d. of George Harding
July 23	Bartholomew s. of John Bradden
Aug. 2	Grace Sandle
Aug. 26	Beniamin s. of Manuel Swetman
Sep. 5	Joh. s. of Mr John Freake
Oct. 7	Robert Huit
Oct. 20	Robert Ryall, the elder
Nov. 3	Joane d. of Richard Young
Nov. 6	Marie d. of William Rowles
Jan. 6	Abraham s. of Edmund Swetman
Nov. 30	Thomas Edwards
Jan. 21	Joane d. of James Stroude
Feb. 5	Alice d. of Robert Jaques
Feb. 25	Francis Sandle
Mar. 19	Jane d. of John Humphries

* So in original.

1655.

Mar. 29	William s. of John Welch
June 14	Elizabeth d. of Manuel Swetmau
July 4	Susanna w. of John Humphries
Nov. 1	Thomas Ryall

1656.

April 20	Joane Edwards, widdow
June 18	Charles s. of Mr Charles Croke
June 22	Roger Opie
June 27	Elizabeth d. of George Harding
Sep. 11	Lucie Dowdin, widdow
Sep. 17	William Gibson
Mar. 9	John Cuffe

1657.

May 13	Joseph s. of Richard Young
July 25	Jane d. of George Tite
Aug. 27	Mrs Susan Goddard, widdow
Dec. 21	Abraham s. of Edmund Swetman
Dec. 14	Walter Brittaine
Feb. 25	Thomas s. of [blank] Walters

1658.

Oct. 26	Edith d. of Alexander Greene
Nov. 4	George Tite
Nov. 29	George s. of Thomas Perrie
Mar. 6	Susanna d. of Edward Edwards

1659.

April 13	Walter Brittaine's widdow
May 19	Francis s. of Alexander Adams
Feb. 10	Jane d. of Richard Young
Feb. 15	William Toope
Mar. 21	Joane d. of Richard Young

1660.

April 1	Widdow Saul
June 4	Susanna Still, widdow
July 10	Marie w. of Peter Sandle
Aug. 22	Susanna d. of Thomas Stile
Dec. 2	Vincent Pahner
Jan. 6	John Board
Jan. 8	Elizabeth d. of John Humphries
Jan. 24	Joane d. of Mathew Combes
Feb. 7	Roger Stile

1661.

April 16	Mathew Sandle
May 14	Roger s. of James Stroud
July 27	Thomas s. of Edmund Swetnam
Aug. 29	Thomas s. of Timothie Sandle
Oct. 18	Abraham s. of Edmund Swetnam
Feb. 4	John Edwards

Mar. 9	George Greene
Mar. 15	James s. of Mathew Combes

1662.

June 9	Joane w. of John Forward
Aug. 25	Marie d. of John Joup
Nov. 3	Thomas s. of Robert Ryall
Jan. 4	Marie d. of Edmund Swetnam
Feb. 16	John Cornish

1663.

Mar. 28	Euerard Slatford
April 23	Edward s. of William Parfoote

1664.

April 4	Mrs Rachel Field w. of Mr Nathaniel Field
May 26	William Hinkstridge
July 4	Thomasine Doggerell
Sep. 15	Elizabeth Dauis w. of John Dauis
Sep. 16	Marie w. of Richard Bayly
Oct. 4	Joane w. of Robert Ryall
Oct. 19	Francis s. of Francis Joup
Nov. 20	Grace w. of John Stroude
Jan. 2	Richard s. of Richard White
Jan. 24	George s. of John Edwards
Feb. 5	Elenor w. of John Edwards
Feb. 17	Joane w. of Robert Toope

1665.

April 3	Cutbert Trimboy
April 23	John s. of John Edwards
May 11	Mrs [blank] * Stourton w. of Mr William Stourton
July 17	Anne w. of William Bernard
Aug. 2	Elizabeth d. of Robert Sandle
Oct. 23	John Lambe
Nov. 30	Agnes Lambe
Dec. 15	Elizabeth w. of Josias White
Jan. 1	Anne Allford
Jan. 17	William Harding
Mar. 22	Mr Nathaniel Field

1666.

May 2	Walter Board
May 7	John s. of Robert Greene
Oct. 3	Francis Joup & Ann his wife
Dec. 14	Elizabeth w. of Alexander Greene
Feb. 14	Nicholas Perre

1667.

April 23	Renaldo Mounk s. of Renaldo Mounk

* An inscription in the church gives the name Margaret. See Introduction.

Aug. 15	George Butler
Oct. 23	Avis Edwards
Oct. 26	Joane Britten
Dec. 16	Richard Bayly
Jan. 15	Thomas Sandall
Dec. 16	Robt Davis
Jan. 30	Ann Holland
Jan. 30*	John Evell
Feb. 8	Richard Morice
Feb. 29	Margeri Roles
Mar. 2	Joane Cufe
Mar. 17	Mari Bayli
Mar. 21	Francis Cufe
Mar. 21	Joane Braden

1668.

June 8	Leanard Suter
June 29	Avis Lambe
July 28	Ann Presle
Aug. 19	Margret Combe
Nov. 8	Mari Braden
Dec. 2	Jane Paret
Jan. 16	Thomas Tabor
Feb. 1	Dorathi Board

1669.

May 29	Ann Sandall
Aug. 16	Margret Suter
Sep. 11	Mari White
Oct. 26	Nathaniell Evill
Dec. 26	Henr Daunt
Jan. 17	Ann Jupe
Feb. 20	Adam Helier
Feb. 24	Elizabeth Swetnem
Mar. 13	Joane Henstridg

1670.

Mar. 25	Tomsen Sandall
May 7	Elizabeth White
June 12	Basell Smart
July 28	John Presli
July 31	Sarah Suter
Aug. 10	Valentine Petue
Aug. 23	Robert Shepd
Sep. 15	Judith Butler
Sep. 28	Mari Evill
Nov. 20	Caterne Toope

1671.

April 7	Ann Open
Aug. 12	Francis Cufe
Sep. 25	Mathew Combe
Oct. 8	John Bayli
Oct. 11	Elizbeth Ings
Oct. 23	Mr Tho. Coye

* Written on the margin. The writing and spelling from 1666 to end of 1671 are very bad.

Dec. 12	John Paret
Dec. 17	Elizbeth Sandall
Dec. 28	Mr John Derbe, Minester
Dec. 29	Edward Baker

1672.

May 1	Joane w. of James Pearsy*
May 7	The R^t ho^{ble} Lord Will. Stourton†
May 13	Rober Joup
June 15	Henry Jefferys
July 3	Margery Preasly, wid.
July 21	Mary w. of Thos Stone
July 22	Rachell Channon
Aug. 11	John Best
Sep. 27	Mrs Mary Stourton
Oct. 5	Mr Rob. Barnes
Nov. 27	Hester Green w. of George Gre.
Jan. 7	Mrs Rachael Crooke
Feb. 20	Joseph White
Mar. 12	John Presly
Mar. 18	John Umphrys
Mar. 21	John Adams

1673.

May 5	Elizabeth Crooke
May 22	Mary Feltham
July 27	John Forward
Aug. 31	Bassill Sheapard
Sep. 9	Joane Cox
Sep. 24	Margarett Evill
Feb. 18	Elizabeth Leversage

1674.

April 12	Margarett Perry
April 21	Ann Bradden
April 21	Mary Thrimboy
April 25	John Dier
May 3	Elizabeth Bradden
May 10	Elizabeth Parfit
June 5	Tomsen Stroud
June 14	Amy‡ Parfitt
July 4	Robert Royall
July 11	Mary Feltham
July 13	Mr Barnes, widd.
July 18	Christian Odber
Aug. 14	John Joupe
Aug. 16	John Evill
Nov. 16	Francis Parfitt
Dec. 6	Mary Adams }
Dec. 12	Sarah Adams d. }
Dec. 20	Nicholas Bowne
Feb. 10	Alexander Adams
Feb. 28	Robert Green

* D. R. Presly.   † The tenth Baron.
‡ D. R. Ann.

1675.

April 3	Adam Cuffe	
May 10	Thomas Perry	
July 18	John Presly s. of John Presly	
July 30	John Edwards	
Aug. 22	Ann Edwards	
Dec. 7	Elizabeth Stourton	
Dec. 23	Mary Davys	
Dec. 29	Robert Joupe	
Mar. 21	Susan Poore	

1676.

April 5	Elinor Wilkins
April 7	Mary Harte
May 25	Lucy Edwards
June 8	Susan Umphrys
June 10	Peter Sandall
July 3	John Moors
July 5	Elinor Bradden
Aug. 3	Rachell Davis
Aug. 11	Henry Milbarom
Aug. 23	Edith Stroud
Sep. 20	Edith Philips
Oct. 21	Joane Copestake
Nov. 8	Josiahs White
Nov. 22	Dorathy Adams
Dec. 23	Thomas Moors
Jan. 25	Ales Royall
Mar. 5	Thomas Presly

1677.

May 2	Mᵣˢ Mary Crooke
May 26	Adrew Lamb
Aug. 12	Fraces Green
Nov. 18	Tho. Gartrill
Nov. 30	Peter Poore
Jan. 30	Robert Sandall
Feb. 11	Francis Felthomo
Feb. 14	Mᵣ Charles Barnes

1678.

April 18	John Trimboy
Nov. 18	Edward Edwards
Nov. 22	Elizab. Dyer
Jan. 22	Elizb. & Mary Perry*
Mar. 3	John White

1679.

April 11	George Harding
April 27	Margery Evill
May 11	Francis Evill
June 10	Mary Parfitt
Aug. 24	Martha Hart
Sep. 9	William Parfitt
Sep. 12	Julian Suter

* D. R. has Elizab. Pearcy & Mary Perry. See Baptisms, 1678.

Sep. 12	William Richardson
Sep. 14	Mary Sandail
Oct. 12	Ann Forwood
Nov. 10	Tho. Sandall
Dec. 15	Susan & Margarett Poor
Jan. 6	Joan Sweatman
Jan. 21	Martha Stroud
Feb. 15	Thomas Evill
Mar. 6	Mary Green
Mar. 21	Judithe Style

1680.

May 18	James Scott
June 5	John Poore
Sep. 6	John Bradden
Sep. 23	Emanuell Sweatman
Nov. 23	Richard Wadly
Dec. 7	John Sandall
Feb. 18	Abigall Bucher
Feb. 23	Nicholas Dyer
Mar. 11	Elizabeth Ferry [or Percy]

1681.

Mar. 30	John White

[A blank space is left for the rest of this year. There is no return to be found in the D. R.]

1682.

May 10	Isaake Sheapard
Sep. 1	Edward Sweatman
Nov. 12	Thomas Style
Dec. 18	William Poore
Dec. 31	Frances Hart
Jan. 14	Phillip Barnes
Jan. 19	Margaret Moores
Feb. 11	Peter Poore
Mar. 1	Thomas Moores

1683.

May 28	William Joupe
June 8	Mary Perman
June 19	John Poore
Sep. 3	Mary Sheapard
Oct. 25	Mary Poore
Dec. 6	Morrice Barnes
Dec. 11	Thomas Gartrill
Dec. 16	John White
Dec. 28	John Sandall
Mar. 12	William Parfitt

1684.

April 5	William Evil s. of John
April 11	Elizabeth Sweatman

May 29   John Green
Aug. 25   [blank] Barnett, of Meere*

1691.

April 20   Mr Matthew Stourton
May 29   Elizabeth Parfitt
Aug. 26   Charles Bisse
Sep. 15   William Green
Sep. 19   Mr Joseph Gildon
Oct. 18   Thomas Stone
Nov. 9   Robert Barrons
Nov. 9   Clare Bracher

1692.

Mar. 28   Christopher Wi'dsor
April 4   Mary Davis
June 6   Susannah Young
July 14   Sarah Strowd
July 14   Christian Barber
July 29   John Sweatman
Aug. 22   William Sandall
Oct. 6   Robert Bennet
Oct. 13   William Davis
Nov. 20   Grace Swetman
Feb. 28   James Meaden

1693.

April 19   Mary Sandall
April 23   Jane Duffitt
May 9   Catherine Sandall
Nov. 10   Ann Palmer
Dec. 9   Grace Jones
Jan. 1   George Phillips
Jan. 19   Elizabeth Frith
Jan. 19   Edward Suter

1694.

April 15   Avis Baker
April 20   Sarah Sandall
Aug. 5   Margaret Brimson
Aug. 14   Ann Whadly†
Aug. 27   William Inngs
Sep. 1   Rich. Bayly
Oct. 6   Ann Sweatman
Oct. 13   Mary Reed
Oct. 19   Ann Russell
Nov. 6   Tomasin Taboure
Nov. 15   Rueth Welch
Nov. 16   Jame Childs
Nov. 19   Hannah Barns

* The first Register book ends here, and the second book begins in 1691. A leaf has evidently been cut out at some time. Sir R. C. Hoare, in 'Modern Wilts,' quotes an entry of Burial of William, Baron Stourton, in Aug. 1685; but he may have derived it only from an inscription in the church. See Introduction.
† D. R. Wadly.

Nov. 27   Mary Barnett
Dec. 5   Elizabeth Perry [or Percy]
Dec. 7   John Umphrys
Dec. 7   Cicily Davis
Dec. 22   Jo.* Owen
Jan. 29   John Sweatman
Feb. 1   John Hart
Feb. 16   William Odber
Feb. 17   Charles Davis
Feb. 20   Avis Chinnok
Feb. 25   William Target

1695.

May 28   John Sheapard
June 30   Joane Sweatman
[blank]   Jane Duffit
May ?   Jerom Edwards
Nov. 17   James Godden†
Dec. 2   Magd Adams
Jan. 27   Michell Target
Mar. ?   Bassill Cuffe, wid.

1696.

April 1   Mary Feltham
April 7   Mary Parfitt
Aug. 4   John Sandall
Aug. 14   John Godden
Sep. 6   Ann Slatford, wid.
Sep. 16   Joan Moores
Nov. 9   Joan Sweatman
Nov. 25   Mary Sparrow
Dec. 12   Rob. Wilmott
Jan. 1   Elizabert Combs
Feb. 6   Mary Barber
Feb. 15   Alce White
Feb. 26   John Lamb
Mar. 3   John Sheapard
Mar. 16   Ms Grace Slatford

1697.

April 17   Mr John Waram‡
May 3   Thomas Cooke
May 12   Mary Winsor
Oct. 18   Elizabeth Joupe
Jan. 7   Thomas Wilkins
Feb. 3   Charles Davis
Feb. 4   Edith Styles
Feb. 15   Mr Thomas Cox
Feb. 15   Alce Meaden

1698.

Mar. 27   Joyce Ryall
May 15   Mary Roles
May 24   Selina Cuffe
Aug. 11   William Moores

* D. R. John.   † D. R. Thomas Godwin.
‡ D. R. Warrum.

Dec. 22	Mꝰ Dorathy Drew
Jan. 11	Mʳ Walter Barns
Jan. 22	John Baker

1699.

April 7	John Tabor
June 21	John Sheapard
June 22	Francis Joupe
Nov. 30	John Michell
Dec. 31	John Perry
Jan. 31	Edith Sheapard
Mar. 7	William Mills

1700.

April 1	John Dyer
April 11	Elizabeth Sandall
May 9	Mꝰ Joan Moore
May 13	Elizabeth Thrimboy
July 2	Grace Godden
Aug. 29	Alice Green, vid.
Nov. 24	Robert Toope
Feb. 1	Elizabeth Combs, vid.
Mar. 1	Frances Davis
Mar. 20	Timothy Sandall
Mar. 23	John Evill
Mar. 25	John Brickle

1701.

Mar. 29	Isaak Sheapard
Mar. 30	John Joupe
April 7	Mary Sheapard
April 27	Robert Throaks
Aug. 9	Elizab. Barns, wid.
Oct. 22	John Atkins
Dec. 11*	John Byflet
Jan. 22	Robert Feltham
Feb. 10	Robert Joupe
Mar. 19	Rose Ryall
Mar. 22	Francis Reed

1702.

Mar. 29	Barbara Toope, wid.
April 16	Robert Childs
May 16	Elizabeth Green
Aug. 30	Robert Godden
Dec. 10	Richard Brickle
Dec. 21	Thomas & Joane Smith
Jan. 17	William Jenkins

1703.

May 3	William Byflet
July 6	Cicily Evill
July 25	Elizabeth Mayo
Feb. 27	Ann Charetou†

* D. R. omits all entries in this year up to
this date, except that of Elizab. Barns, which is
dated Oct. 22.
† D. R. Charleton.

1704.

April 30	Robert Rial
May 31	Stephen Smith
Aug. 6	Joseph Barber
Aug. 9	Richard Green
Aug. 10	Widdow Thrimbe
Oct. 8	James Meadon

1705.

April 30	Thomas Haskett
May 13	Will. Baker
Aug. 20	John Smart
Sep. 27	Christopher Target, Junʳ
Nov. 25	Jane Stroud
Dec. 3	Stephen Braddon
Jan. 2	Walter Reed
Jan. 3	Mary Cains
Jan. 15	Mary Tabor
Feb. 23	John s. of John Shuter
Mar. 10	Rachel Sweatman, widdow

1706.

April 9	Alice Edwards, widdow
Aug. 19	Charles Evil
Aug. 24	Mary Willmott
Sep. 15	James s. of John Baker
Oct. 31	Mary w. of John Statford
Dec. 1	Thomas Owen
Feb. 5	Robert Atkins
Mar. 3	Mꝛˢ Joan Davis
Mar. 18	Susan Guyer

1707.

April 25	Mʳ John Stourton
July 20	John Joupe
Sep. 23	Robert Shepherd
Oct. 1	Mꝛˢ Bridget Stourton
Nov. 16	Rebeckah w. of Willᵐ Shepherd
Nov. 26	Joan Perry
Dec. 6	Thomas s. of John Holly
Jan. 28	John s. of Willᵐ Maidman
Jan. 31	Peter King
Feb. 8	Benjamin White

1708.

May 22	Francis Feltham alias Barnes
May 23	Joan Garret, of Killmington
May 30	Hannah w. of Robert Toope
Aug. 30	Ruth Sweatman
Sep. 24	Rose King, widow
Sep. 28	Thomas Mawham
Nov. 13	Martha Feltham
Nov. 24	Sarah Gibbens
Nov. 26	Alice Green, widow

1709.

April 1	George Edwards
April 30	Robert Addams

L

July	17	Francis Jupe
Dec.	26	Rachel King
Jan.	16	James Stone
Feb.	16	Peter King
Mar.	7	John Barber, of Wittam Frairy

1710.

April	12	Robert White
April	12	Joseph Barber, of Wittam Frairy
April	24	John Slatford, of Wittam Frairy
May	4	Anne Lauford
July	24	Christopher Target
Aug.	2	John Bartlet
Aug.	20	Bassil Shepherd
Nov.	4	Mary w. of Will⁰ Richardson
Nov.	24	Mary Bradden, wid.
Jan.	12	Anne w. of Xtopher Welsh
Feb.	14	Catherine Shepherd, wid.
Feb.	19	Jane w. of Thomas Mayo
Mar.	19	Mary d. of John Michel

1711.

Mar.	30	Alice Brickel, wid.
April	3	George s. of Mr John Drew
April	6	Ruth Gover
April	16	Catherine Smart, wid.
June	5	Mrs Catherine Gilden
July	29	Mary Hunt, of Brewham
Aug.	2	John Hill
Aug.	7	Joan Parfit w. of Jerom
Oct.	7	Mary Read
Dec.	30	Thomas White
Jan.	28	Mr John Besely
Feb.	2	Mary Barnet
Mar.	15	Wilfiam s. of Will' Miles
Mar.	23	Robert Davies
Mar.	23	William Duthwait

1712.

April	10	Francis Jupe
May	17	John s. of William Bemman, of Brewham
June	7	Will. s. of Thomas Mayo
July	6	Stephen s. of Stephen Bourton, of Zeals
July	20	John Davis, of Brewham
Sep.	4	Martha Cuff
Sep.	30	Mr Richard Coffin
Oct.	3	Mary d. of Bazil Barber, of Frairy
Oct.	4	Joan w. of Richard Feltham
Oct.	6	Robert s. of Chris. & Joan Target
Oct.	28	Mary Edwards, wid.
Dec.	19	John Jupe

Dec.	21	Elenour Rodway
Dec.	27	Mary w. of Henry Childs
Jan.	12	Joan w. of Thos Tabor
Jan.	12	Agnes d. of Thos Tabor
Jan.	21	Jane w. of John Serrell,* of Silton
Jan.	23	Joan w. of Walter Sparrow
Jan.	23	Joan d. of Thos Tabor
Jan.	26	Joan Jupe, wid.
Feb.	4	Thomas Tabor
Feb.	5	John s. of Thomas Tabor
Feb.	5	Ann Brimson
Feb.	15	Johanna d. of John Heiter, of Zeals
Feb.	23	Susannah d. of Francis & Susannah Jupe
Mar.	10	Edmond Ryal

1713.

April	18	John s. of Robt & Eliz. Alford
May	8	Mrs Margaret Cox
May	16	Walter Sparrow
May	30	William s. of John & Mary Evile
June	30	Ann d. of Will. & Rebeckah Barnet
Sep.	10	Thomas s. of the honble Charles Stourton, Esq., & Catharine his wife
Sep.	13	Mary d. of Elizabeth Gilbert, bas.
Oct.	14	Mary d. of Richd & Eliz. Moor
Oct.	25	Mary Baker
Oct.	25	Thomas s. of Will. & Mary Bracher
Oct.	27	Will. s. of Charles & Jane Evile
Nov.	9	Eliz. d. of Stephen & Mary Collins
Dec.	2	Joan d. of John & Eliz. Bracher

1714.

Mar.	31	Sarah w. of William Meaden
May	13	Mary Lush, widw
June	29	Jerome Parfit
Sep.	17	Rachel d. of Thos & Rachel Charlton, of Zeales
Sep.	23	Ann w. of Ralph Green, of Brewham
Sep.	29	Hannah w. of Robt Green
Jan.	18	William Mitchel
Jan.	18	Eliz. Slatford w. of Joseph Slatford, of Wittam Frayry
Feb.	1	Samuel Lamb

* *Searle* written first and struck out.

1715.

Sep.	4	Aaron s. of Will. & Bridget Green
Oct.	19	Elizabeth Evile, wid*
Jan.	9	Richard Cuff
Mar.	2	William Davis
Mar.	4	Thomas s. of Ann Davis

1716.

May	10	Abraham s. of James & Sarah Cains
May	27	Edith Baker, wid*
Aug.	1	M** Jane Gilden, wid*
Sep.	9	John Presly
Sep.	11	Robert Owen
Oct.	22	Thomas s. of William & Mary King
Dec.	5	Joan d. of John & Joan Baker
Dec.	12	John Hart
Dec.	26	M** Elizabeth Stourton, wid*
Jan.	3	Edward s. of Thomas & Basil Hains
Jan.	31	Henry Humphrys
Mar.	10	Joseph Windsor, of Hindon
Mar.	13	Mary w. of Andrew Shepherd

1717.

May	8	Jane Duthwait, wid*
June	25	William Joup
June	25	Hannah Ingram, of Brewham, wid*
June	29	Robert s. of Richard & Rachel Atkins
July	3	Jane w. of William Brickle
July	13	Cecilia d. of Thomas & Cecilia Green
Aug.	18	William Meaden
Oct.	1	Charles Slatford, of Brewham
Dec.	8	Edith d. of Charles & Catharine Evile
Jan.	3	Melior w. of William Jenkins
Jan.	22	Mary Evile
Feb.	9	Winefrid d. of Thomas & Susanna Cook
Feb.	13	Robert Feltham
Feb.	25	Mary Owen
Feb.	25	Elizabeth d. of Rob* & Lucy Owen
Mar.	2	William Edwards

1718.

April	21	William Tucker
April	27	Miriam w. of John Feltham
Nov.	9	John s. of John & Ann Shepherd
Dec.	25	Mary White

1719

April	2	Luce d. of Thomas & Margery Hurdle
May	25	Nicolas Butcher
May	29	Mary d. of John & Ann Shuter
Aug.	7	Thomas Brewnel
Aug.	20	Edward s. of John & Joan Baker
Aug.	31	William Green
Sep.	23	William Miles
Jan.	2	Sarah d. of William & Mary King
Mar.	9	Bridget d. of William & Bridget Green

1720.

April	20	Richard Atkins
May	25	Ann Jenison, wid*
July	11	Dorothy d. of the Hon*** Charles Stourton, Esq., & Catharine his wife
Nov.	10	Mary d. of William & Mary King
Nov.	17	Mary w. of Hercules Dingerst, of North Bruham
Dec.	5	John Cox
Dec.	21	Margaret Collin
Jan.	9	Eliz. w. of Nicolas Edwards
Feb.	9	Francis Baker
Feb.	10	Bridget w. of William Bracher
Feb.	17	Robert s. of Rich** Feltham
Feb.	23	Eliz. d. of William & Mary Markey
Mar.	9	Susannah Atkins, wid*

1721.

April	19	Frances w. of M* Henery Wall
May	27	Rob* s. of Richard & Rachel Atkins
Aug.	13	Tho* Hunt, of Brewham
Sep.	4	Thomas Golding
Sep.	7	Grace d. of Jeremiah & Grace Target
Sep.	17	Robert Tabour
Jan.	7	Mary w. of Thomas Ryal
Jan.	22	Thomas Presly
Feb.	13	John Cary

1722.

April	3	Thomas Mayo
May	20	Edith d. of Charles & Catharine Evile
June	21	John Barnet
July	1	John Shepherd
July	13	Thomas s. of John & Ann Shepherd
July	15	Dionysia d. of John & Ann Shepherd

Oct. 21	William Brickle	
Nov. 14	Thomas s. of Thomas & Susannah Cook	
Jan. 15	John Phelps, of Lovels Upton	
Jan. 23	Rob¹ Slatford, of Brewham	
Feb. 1	Francis s. of William & Winifred Sweatman	
Feb. 27	Joan w. of John Baker	
Mar. 8	Francis s. of John & Joan Baker	
Mar. 22	Elenour d. of Robert & Eliz. Baker	

1723.

Mar. 27	Mary w. of John Bradden
April 11	William Evile
April 22	Eliz. w. of Rob¹ Alford
May 23	John Trimby
June 2	Grace w. of Edward Edwards
July 7	William Meaden
Aug. 13	Charles Barns
Aug. 25	James Stroud
Nov. 8	Mary Chinnock
Nov. 21	Andrew Shepherd
Dec. 1	Mary d. of Nathaniel & Mary Ireson
Dec. 26	Eliz. d. of James & Eliz. Bracher
Jan. 1	Isit w. of John Mitchell, of Kilminton
Jan. 19	Rob¹ Baker
Jan. 22	Margaret Tabour
Feb. 2	George s. of Eliz. Baker, wid.
Mar. 16	Mary w. of William Edwards
Mar. 20	John Bradden, Sen⁽, of Gasper
Mar. 21	Margaret d. of Thoˢ & Mary Mores
Mar. 22	Jane w. of Rob¹ Toop
Mar. 24	Mary w. of Thoˢ Mores, of Gillingham

1724.

April 28	Mrˢ Hartgale
June 7	Luce w. of Edward Sweatman
June 15	William Maidment
Sep. 6	Jane w. of Charles Evil
Nov. 7	Han'ah d. of Henry & Mary Cooper
Nov. 19	Christable Sandel
Jan. 27	John s. of Robert Alford
Mar. 7	Ruth d. of Charles & Catherine Evil
Mar. 24	Henry Hoare, Esq⁽

1725.

May 1	Basil Cuff
May 18	Mary d. of Willm Combs. of Gasper

May 22	John Edwards
June 7	Joan d. of Jeremiah & Grace Target
Aug. 21	Mary Maidment, widⁿ, of Gasper
Oct. 19	Mr Edmund Wadlo
Dec. 9	Richard s. of John & Joan Baker, Gasp⁽
Dec. 16	Joan w. of John Baker, jun⁽, Gasp⁽
Feb. 15	Frances Sandle w. of Thoˢ Sandle, G⁽
Feb. 17	Eliz. w. of William Bracher, G⁽
Mar. 3	John Baker, sen⁽

1726.

Mar. 29	Edward Edwards
Mar. 29	William Edwards
June 13	Elisha s. of James & Dorothy Sandle
July 8	James Sandle
July 10	Robert Green
Aug. 7	William s. of Willm Bratcher
Aug. 9	William Maidment
Sep. 30	Joan Poor
Oct. 14	Katherine Shepherd
Oct. 20	John Meaden
Nov. 4	William Cuff
Dec. 30	Mary w. of Richᵈ Feltom
Jan. 1	Jane d. of Henry & Mary Cooper
Jan. 10	Mary Bratcher
Mar. 12	Paul Sandle
Mar. 15	Mrˢ Barnes, widᵂ
Mar. 16	The Honblᵉ Mrˢ Ann Hoare
Mar. 17	Catherine w. of William Moores

1727.

April 24	Mrˢ Coffin*
June 2	Alexander Green
June 19	Mr John Butcher
Sep. 4	William Bratcher†
Oct. 23	Widᵂ Prestley
Nov. 24	Jane Edwards
Dec. 31	Stephen Owen
Jan. 17	John s. of John Web
Feb. 24	William Shepherd
Mar. 5	Martha Line

1728.

April 23	Elizabeth w. of John Bradden
June 21	Susan'a w. of John Miles
Aug. 5	Robert Maidment
Aug. 30	Ann w. of Rob¹ Owen
Sep. 27	William Barnett

* Interlined.
† Bradshaw written first and altered.

Oct. 4   Ann Gilbert
Nov. 28   Dorothy Hart, wid^w
Dec. 2   The Rev^d M^r [blank] Cox
Dec. 23   Mary Collins
Jan. 7   Robert Toop
Jan. 14   [blank]* the w. of John Smart
Jan. 24   Henry Childs
Feb. 7   [blank] the w. of Henry Perfect
Feb. 18   Elizabeth Baker, wid^w
Feb. 19   Richard Evil
Mar. 12   Lucy Owen & Mary Owen herd.
Mar. 17   Mary Joupe, widow
Mar. 18   Joan Targett, widow

1729.

Mar. 26   Ann Bradding,† widow
April 2   Elizabeth w. of Willm Brimson
April 12   Ann d. of John & Ann Edwards
April 17   Robert Barnes
April 24   William Janes
April 24   John Deacons
April 27   Diana Arnold
April 29   Mary Sweatman
May 26‡   Ann Stephens
May 29   Grace Baker
June 10   Joan Owen§
June 15   Robert Owen
July 28   Richard Hill
Sep. 11   Mary Mulbery
Sep. 30   Mary w. of William Jupe
Oct. 20   Edith Evil, wid^w
Oct. 27   Dorothy w. of Francis Sweatman
Nov. 4   John s. of John & Frances Trowbridge
Nov. 15   George s. of George & Elizabeth Green
Nov. 24   Charles s. of Edward & Basil Edwards
Dec. 10   Thomas Cook§
Dec. 12   Ann George, wid^w§
Jan. 13   Samuel Bradshaw
Jan. 31   Jane d. of William & Mary Markey
Mar. 24   Frances Davis

1730.

April 26   Anastacia w. of Edward Edwards
May 22   William Richardson
Sep. 3   Frances Harden
Feb. 7   Charles Feltom

* D. R. Mary.   † D. R. Bradden.
‡ D. R. has May 7, Thomas Davidge; and omits all the rest in this year.
§ Interlined.

1731.

April 7   John Pin alias Holly
Aug. 30   Mary late w. of John White
Sep. 1   Joan Feltom
Dec. 6   Lætitia Evans, of Zeals
Dec. 27   William Moors

1732.

May 5   William Marnal
May 23   John Bradden
June 18   James Kains, of Long Lane Mill
June 27   Mrs Bridget Coffin
July 23   Agnes Hunt, of Frary
Aug. 17   Thomas Green
Sep. 11   Agatha Smart, of Wincanton
Sep. 13   Mr Harry Wall
Jan. 5   Eleanor Jupe

1733.

April 1   Jane d. of William & Mary Markey
April 18   Ann w. of William Edwards
May 24   Thomas Sandal
June 17   Joan Sheppard, wid^w
Aug. 12   William Brickle
Aug. 13   Francis Sweatman
Aug. 23   William Banister
Sep. 27   John Rodaway
Jan. 24   Thomas Ryal

1734.

June 3   Elizabeth late w. of James Bratcher
Sep. 26   Jane Arnold
Sep. 27   Hannah d. of Charles & Dorothy Evil
Oct. 13   Henry Lockier*
Oct. 17   Betty d. of Charles & Catharine Evil
Oct. 21   Thomas Target
Nov. 10   Clara d. of James Bratcher
Nov. 13   William Sweatman
Mar. 11   Thomas Miles

1735.

June 12   Robert Tabor, Junr
July 30   Alice Barnes
Oct. 15   Frances d. of [blank] White
Jan. 30   Miss Ann Hoare

1736.

Aug. 1   Richard Moors
Aug. 31   Mary Pond
Mar. 23   Mary Jupe

* Interlined.

1737.

May	6	Bridget White
Nov.	26	William s. of James Keens
Dec.	18	John Pond
Mar.	3	Sarah d. of Joseph & Hanna Stone

1738.

May	10	Elizabeth Ridgley
Aug.	11	Edmund Wadloe
Oct.	31	John Suter
Nov.	6	Mary w. of John Shepherd
Dec.	20	Ann Brickle, widᵂ
Jan.	27	Susanna d. of William & Susanna Moors
Feb.	13	Mʳ Richard Collin
Mar.	3	Robert s. of George & Elizabeth Green
Mar.	18	Andrew Top

1739.

April	9	William Childs
April	12	Jane d. of Robert Smart
April	21	Mary d. of John Bradden, Junʳ
April	27	Mr Thomas Davis
May	22	Mary w. of John Edwards
Sep.	12	Catharine Slatford, widᵂ
Sep.	18	William Brimson
Nov.	13	Ruth Jupe w. of William Jupe, of Zeals
Dec.	13	Humphry Scammel
Jan.	20	Elizabeth w. of James Bull

1740.

May	6	Dulce Trimby
Aug.	3	Charles Evil
Aug.	14	John Feltom
Jan.	6	Susanna Cook
Jan.	11	Susanna Atkins
Jan.	30	Jane Bowls

1741.

May	23	Mary Owen, yᵉ foundling child
Aug.	16	Henry Cooper
Aug.	18	Edith Cooper
Aug.	23	Ann Evil
Aug.	24	James Land
Sep.	11	Ann Shepherd
Sep.	19	Sarah Barnet
Sep.	25	John Bratcher
Oct.	10	Thomas Barnet*
Oct.	17	Mary Jupe
Oct.	27	Ruth Feltom
Nov.	14	Alice Target
Nov.	23	James Bratcher
Dec.	30	Edmund Wadloe

* Interlined.

Jan.	4	Elizabeth w. of Joseph Millar
Jan.	12	William Deacons

1742.

April	11	Mary w. of John Green
May	17	Jane Slatford
June	25	Mʳˢ Jane Hoare
Sep.	16	Elizabeth Dibbin
Oct.	25	Joshua Davis
Oct.	26	John Laws
Oct.	31	Sarah Meaden
Nov.	7	John Deacons
Nov.	17	Mary w. of John Jupe
Nov.	26	Ann Wadloe*
Nov.	27	Elizabeth Feltom
Nov.	27	John Brickle
Dec.	24	John Bradden
Dec.	30	Mary Keins
Jan.	5	Margaret Miles
Jan.	8	John Shepherd
Jan.	9	Margery Hurdle
Jan.	13	Thomas Target
Jan.	27	Jane Smart
Jan.	28	Edward Edwards
Feb.	6	Mary Baker
Feb.	13	James Bradshaw

1743.

Mar.	29	Mary White
April	8	John Baker
May	1	Mʳˢ Susanna Hoare*
May	17	Harry Edwards
June	1	Ann Holly
June	9	William Beaumont
June	17	Gertrude Jupe
June	17	Elizabeth Beaumont
Jan.	6	James Bradden
Jan.	9	Samuel Lamb
Jan.	25	Mary w. of Thomas Tabor
Jan.	25	Thomas Tabor, their son

1744.

April	1	The Honᵇˡᵉ Thomas, Lord Stourton†
May	10	John s. of William Feltom
May	17	Mary w. of William Combs
June	10	Elizabeth Frith
Sep.	16	The Widᵂ Ann Baker, of Bourton
Nov.	23	Mary Collins
Dec.	12	Elizabeth Shepherd, widᵂ
Dec.	12	Thomas Edwards
Dec.	21	Sarah Bratcher
Jan.	24	Martha Owen

* Interlined.
† The thirteenth Baron, born 1677, and succeeded his brother Edward in 1720.

Feb. 12	Joan Alford	
Mar. 15	Richard Edwards	

1745.

Mar. 27	Stephen Collins
May 1	Jane Edwards
May 26	John Edwards
June 2	[blank] * Haynes
Aug. 27	James Meaden
Aug. 31	Rebecca Jackson†
Sep. 1	Sarah Keins
Sep. 6	Rebecca d. of John Jackson
Jan. 6	Mrs Jane Davis
Jan. 14	Edward Sweatman
Feb. 8	Bridget Bratcher
Feb. 28	Elizabeth d. of William Jupe

1746.

April 27	William Moor
May 8	Mary w. of John Hill
June 14	William Jupe
Aug. 28	Thomas Moores
Sep. 28	Robert Alford
Nov. 28	Rebecca Barnett
Jan. 6	John Smart
Mar. 9	Susanna w. of Francis Jupe, of Stoke
Mar. 13	Catharine w. of Joseph Lampard
Mar. 17	Mary w. of Thomas Lampard

1747.

July 13	Mary w. of Stephen Penny
Nov. 10	Mary w. of John Jackson
Nov. 17	William Jupe
Jan. 22	Elizabeth w. of Robert Tabor
Mar. 2	Margaret Holly, wid^w

1748.

April 15	Edward Edwards
May 22	Charles Edwards
June 12	Charles s. of John Evil
June 13	William Jupe, of Zeals
June 18	Rachel w. of Richard Atkins, the elder
June 28	[blank] s. of Morice & Mary Walter
July 10	Martha d. of Basil Edwards
Sep. 24	Michael Brimson
Oct. 13	James Hilleker
Oct. 18	William Combs
Nov. 8	Joshua Edwards
Dec. 13	Hannah Feltom
Jan. 12	William Evelle‡

* D. R. Basil.
† This entry has been partially struck out, and probably relates to the same burial as that dated Sep. 6.   ‡ Altered to Evil.

Jan. 25	Rachel Charleton
Jan. 28	John Mitchel

1749.

June 9	Edward Parsons Paps
June 19	The Honble Elizabeth, Lady Stourton
June 22	Elizabeth Brimson
June 26	James Hilliker
June 28	Ann Lamb, widow
Aug. 16	Ann Bratcher
Sep. 7	John Evil
Oct. 19	Sarah Dixs
Nov. 7	James Sparrow
Dec. 1	Mary Meaden, widow
Feb. 14	Charles Evil

1750.

April 3	Robert Taber
Aug. 2	Hannah w. of Joseph Stone
Nov. 30	Mrs Margaret Crowthorne
Dec. 13	Phan'ey Curtis
Dec. 29	Ann Street, of Zeals
Jan. 26	Ann Curtis d. of ye afores^d Phaney Curtis
Feb. 3	John s. of Thomas & Sarah Taber
Feb. 13	John Target
Mar. 22	George Green

1751.

Nov. 11	Harry Baker
Dec. 11	Martha Target

1752.

Jan. 7	William Markey
Jan. 15	Mary w. of William Bratcher, sen^r
April 23	Elizabeth Moors, widow
May 20	Francis Shepherd
June 19	Edward Bennet
July 4	Mary Ransom*
Sep. 15	Stephen Penny
Oct. 1	Elizabeth Goldin w. of Robert Goldin
Oct. 14	Ann w. of Richard Atkins
Nov. 3	Thomas Blake
Dec. 8	Cecilia Green, widow
Dec. 24	Mary Miles, widow

1753.

Jan. 26	Mary Cains
Mar. 25	Mary late w. of Joseph Stone, jun^r
April 15	Henery Baker
April 26	Elizabeth Rolls

* Original has after this entry "new stile."

June 22	Susanna d. of William & Susanna Moors	June 18	Jane Stone
July 19	The Honble Lady Winifred late w. of Lord William Stourton	Sep. 8	[blank] Bratcher, from the workhouse
		Sep. 20	Elizabeth Godden. from d^o, an Infant, drown'd
Aug. 16	Mary Green, alias Baker	Oct. 1	Mary Sandal (a Papist)
Oct. 4	Robert Baker, of Bourton		
Nov. 1	Elias s. of James Meaden		1758.
Nov. 17	Mary Edwards		
Dec. 30	Joseph Stone	Jan. 19	Walter Barnes, a Papist
		Feb. 17	Elizabeth Target
	1754.	Mar. 10	Ruth Moores, from the workhouse
Feb. 22	Barbary Odford	May 4	Mary Barker, of Knoyle
Feb. 26	James Atkins	Aug. 16	Sarah Stone, from the workhouse
Mar. 5	Mrs Grace Hill		
April 21	Charles Evil	Aug. 27	Mary Baker, from the workhouse
June 5	Eleonar Edwards		
Aug. 6	Thomas Knight	Dec. 11	Mary Bradden
Aug. 31	The Revd Mr John Hill	Nov. 21	James Kaines, a Papist
Nov. 10	William Smart		
			1759.
	1755.	Feb. 9	Dorothy Evile
Mar. 3	Mary Evile	Feb. 9	Richd Portnel, from ye workhouse
Mar. 20	William Atkins		
April 16	Rachael Edwards	April 5	Mary w. of Matthew Davis, a Papist
May 16	Robert Godwin		
June 25	Mary a child of Ann Clements	May 3	George Edwards, Top Lane
Aug. 1	Catherine Evile, of Black Slough	July 21	William Feltham
		June 3	Robert Miles
Aug. 31	Jane Smart	July 7	Mary w. of John Owen, Junr
		July 25	Sarah Burree
	1756.	Aug. 15	John Owen, Junr
Mar. 20	Mrs Dorothy Barton	May 10	Mrs Ann Hoare
April 26	Catherine Orchard	Sep. 6	Grace Target, Tucking Mills
May 12	John Baker	Oct. 24	Mary Gover, widow
May 21	Sarah Bond	Nov. 1	Robert Feltham (an Infant), Papist
May 25	Jonathan Stone		
July 11	Mary Cooper, from ye workhouse	Nov. 3	Ann w. of John Target
		Dec. 19	Charles Arnold, an Infant
Aug. 22	Ann Wallow, a child		
Sep. 4	John Target		1760.
Sep. 17	Francis Jupe, of South Brewham	Jan. 2	Catherine Evil, widow
		Jan. 4	Sarah Bradden, an Infant
Sep. 20	Mary Owen	Jan. 9	Michael Tottershall, a Papist
Nov. 28	Ann Baker	Feb. 16	John Orchard
Dec. 23	Ann Dorothy Barton, an Infant	April 27	Mark Shepheard, a Papist
		May 3	Dorothy Miles, widow
	1757.	May 24	John an illegitimate s. of Mary Holley
Jan. 11	Jeremiah Target		
Jan. 13	Mary Green	Oct. 5	Esther Davis, a Papist
Feb. 11	George Edwards, of Stourton Lane	Dec. 2	Ann Clements, from ye workhouse
Feb. 25	David Boyt, from ye workhouse		1761.
Mar. 1	William Edwards, from Black Slough	Feb. 7	John Bradden, sen^r
		Mar. 1	Mary Bradshaw, widow
June 9	Ann Dibbin, from the workhouse	Aug. 7	Jonas Parfect
		April 30	Richard Atkins, from ye workhouse
June 10	William Green, an Infant		

May	5	M⁰ˢ Ann Whitaker
Aug.	28	Abigail Target
Sep.	7	Joseph Bond
Sep.	25	John Targett
Oct.	31	Edward Edwards, from yᵉ workhouse
Dec.	13	William Target, an Infant

1762.

Jan.	20	Francis Edwards, an Infant
Feb.	26	James s. of William Markey
May	5	Mary w. of John Evill
July	29	Tomasin Pearce, from Silton
Aug.	7	William Moors, junʳ
Sep.	25	James Whitaker
Dec.	25	M⁰ˢ Jane Cornelisen, widow *

1763.

Mar.	21	Ann w. of David Boyte
April	24	William Bond, senior
June	7	Dorothy Miles, an Infant

1764.

Feb.	9	Mary Markey, widow
April	11	William Hayter
April	29	Ann Doulton, an Infant
May	26	[blank] Davis, an Infant, a Papist
May	30	John Green
June	6	James Parfit, a boy from Zeals, killed by a fall from a tree at Bonham†
Aug.	12	Thomas Burree, junʳ
Oct.	1	Thomas Swain
Oct.	6	Martha Target
Oct.	31	Jane Lapham

1765.

Mar.	18	Mary Sparrow
Mar.	22	Joan Boreton, a Papist
July	3	Jane Bratcher, a Papist, from yᵉ workhouse
Aug.	6	William Bratcher, a Papist, aged 95
Aug.	13	Ann Markey
Aug.	22	Francis Jupe
Sep.	29	Robert Smart, from the workhouse
Nov.	3	William & Ann Frith, from the workhouse
Nov.	23	John Turner, kill'd by yᵉ fall of a piece of timber from yᵉ Temple of the Sun‡
Dec.	1	Felix Edwards, an Infant

* Eldest da. of the first Henry Hoare, of Stourhead.
† Interlined.
‡ An ornamental building in the pleasure grounds at Stourhead.

1766.

Jan.	12	Philip Markey
Feb.	4	Mary Arnold
Mar.	5	Samuel Whitaker, an Infant
Mar.	18	Betty Curtis, an Infant
April	13	Elizabeth Combes, an Infant
April	20	John Target, senʳ
April	22	Martin Jupe, an Infant
May	7	Elizabeth Green, an Infant
May	8	John White, Butcher
May	21	Mʳ Richard Molineux, a Popish Priest, from Bonham
May	22	George Green, an Infant
Aug.	9	Grace Edwards, from yᵉ workhouse
Aug.	31	Susannah Bradden
Sep.	21	John Miles* (Mʳ Hoare's groom), aged 24
Sep.	26	John Evil,* aged 20 ⎫ Brother
Sep.	28	Mary Evil,* aged 16 ⎬ and
Sep.	30	Betty Evil,* aged 18 ⎭ sisters
Oct.	2	Cornelius Shepherd, aged 71
Nov.	22	Susannah Moores, aged 60
Dec.	19	Robert Shepherd, aged 78

1767.

July	12	Rachael Edwards, from yᵉ workhouse, aged 51
July	20	Thomas Evil, an Infant
Oct.	2	Ann Feltham, a Papist, aged 45
Nov.	1	Dorcas Swain, aged 86
Dec.	26	William Burree, an Infant

1768.

Feb.	7	Susannah Feltham, aged 32
Feb.	9	Thomas Rial, aged 70
Feb.	9	Edward Rial, an Infant
Mar.	17	Elizabeth Edwards, aged 87
Mar.	26	James Smart, an Infant
April	19	Jane Green, an Infant
May	21	Mʳˢ Jane Crooke, a Papist, aged 66
June	9	John Dullit, from yᵉ workhouse, aged 85
June	28	Mary Markey, æt. 38
July	5	Joan Bratcher (78)
Nov.	8	Basil Edwards (58)
Nov.	27	Catherine Gorland (80)
Dec.	11	John Edwards (76)

1769.

Mar.	8	Sarah Target (35)
April	3	Dorothy Jupe (79)
April	29	Richard Arnold (66)
May	26	Mary Davidge, a Papist (66)

* "These died of ulcerous sorethroats."

M

June 9	Jonathan Meaden, from Bourton (65)	
July 4	William Elmes, an Infant	
July 30	Leah Evill, an Infant	
Sep. 5	Charles Feltham, a Papist (19)	
Sep. 24	Richard Rial, an Infant	
Oct. 8	Joseph Target (25)	
Oct. 22	Sarah Stacey, from Motcombe (28)	
Nov. 9	John Wadlow (54)	

1770.

Mar. 3	James Ingram (12)
Mar. 10	Esther Ingram (5)
April 10	Mary Combes (40)
May 29	Elizabeth Feltham (62)
June 10	Silas Bracher, an Infant
July 29	John Trimby, sen^r (56)
Aug. 7	Edward Lampard, an Infant
Aug. 28	William Miles, an Infant
Dec. 4	Mrs Mary Pyke, a Papist (80)

1771.

Mar. 24	Jame Lapham (50)
April 29	Jane Green, an Infant
May 15	Martha Bradden (20)
May 28	Mary Edwards (84)
June 23	William Target (37)
June 27	William Lawes (31)
Sep. 1	Martha Green (14)
Oct. 6	Betty Philips (88)
Nov. 10	Mary Holly (68)

1772.

Jan. 5	Betty Edwards (84)
Feb. 9	Ann Tabor, an Infant
Mar. 5	John Owen (76)
Mar. 11	Ann Lapham (50), S^l Pox
April 8	Sarah Baker (35)
April 26	Thomas Feltham, an Infant
May 13	Mr John Hill (82)
June 21	Betty Combes (48)
July 22	Edward Bracher (25)
Aug. 1	Thomas Burree (80)
Aug. 7	Ann Lapham (57)
Sep. 30	Mary Meaden (70)
Dec. 20	Thomas Markey, an Infant

1773.

Jan. 14	Thomas Shepherd, an Infant
Jan. 30	Mary Miles (40)
Feb. 11	Samuel Edwards (55)
Feb. 11	John Baker, an Infant
Feb. 14	Elizabeth Arnold (72)
Mar. 7	Richd Bradden, an Infant
Mar. 22	James Jupe, an Infant
April 5	Rachel Meaden (63), from Bourton

April 6	Edith Feltham (72)
April 17	Ann Lapham (30)
May 18	Mrs Mary Barnes (82), a Papist
July 18	Hannah Lawes (57)
July 25	Richard Lapham (87)
Aug. 10	Sarah Tabor (56)

1774.

Mar. 13	Ann Edwards Lapham, an Infant
April 16	Thomas Hurle (88)
April 17	John Edwards (84)
May 15	Thomas Tabor (73), Parish Clerk
May 29	Anne Whitaker, an Infant
June 25	Mary Odbar, a Papist (29)
June 30	Joan Smart (75)
Nov. 4	John Howey, an Infant

1775.

Mar. 12	Jane Baker, an Infant
April 18	Mary Green, a Papist (44)
May 17	Martha Spencer (73)
June 1	John Jupe (62)
July 31	Ann Tabor, an Infant
Oct. 10	John Norris, an Infant
Dec. 17	Elizabeth Hiscock (65)

1776.

Jan. 5	Mary Howey (48)
Mar. 11	Mary Kaines (81), a Papist
Mar. 11	Martha Shepherd (75), a Papist
April 5	Lucy Miles (75)
April 8	William Markey (55)
April 17	Elizabeth Kaines (35)
April 25	Martha Stone, Papist (51)
Aug. 10	William Hilliar (48)
Oct. 20	Lewis Meaden, an Infant
Dec. 15	Betty Clements, an Infant

1777.

Jan. 19	Susanna Combes, an Infant
Mar. 20	Willm Swaine
April 4	Mrs Mary Wadlow (84)
April 5	John Odbar (48), a Papist
April 27	George Norris, an Infant
June 22	Charles Smart, an Infant
June 25	Willm Combes (16)
July 29	Elizabeth Green (85)
Aug. 2	Ann Bradshaw, a Papist (63)
Aug. 10	Hannah Norris, from Kilmington (24)
Aug. 10	Mary Jefferys, from Brewham (47)
Oct. 12	Frances Penny (77)
Oct. 29	William Odbar, a Papist (74)
Nov. 12	Martha Feltham, an Infant

1778.

Feb.	1	Richard Coward (30)
Feb.	22	James Coward, an Infant
Feb.	25	Eleanor Jupe (83)
Mar.	9	Stephen Penny (67)
Mar.	23	Matthew Coombs (57)
April	4	Harriot Turner (5), Burnt
May	1	Mary Smart (60)
May	5	Thomas White, a Papist
May	10	Mary Coward (26)
May	24	Ann Bratcher (40)
July	5	Felix Bratcher, an Infant
July	12	Sarah Bratcher, an Infant, drown'd
Aug.	5	Charlotte Elmes, an Infant
Nov.	21	Luke Markey, an Infant

1779.

Jan.	2	Samuel Lamb (37), from Boreton
Jan.	24	Sarah Yetman, an Infant
Jan.	31	Jane Coombs (50)
Feb.	28	Joseph Feltham, an Infant
Mar.	8	Jane Miles (76)
Mar.	22	David Boyte, sen' (78)
June	24	William Miles (50), from Froome
July	29	John Davis, an Infant, Papist
Aug.	4	Joseph Davis (15), a Papist
Aug.	7	Samuel Lamb (65), from Boreton
Sep.	17	Martha & Richard Bradden, Infants
Oct.	14	Susanna Markey (15)
Nov.	11	Sarah Arnold (39)*
Nov.	12	James Markey (61)
Dec.	3	Mary Green, an Infant

1780.

Jan.	6	Ann Davis (3), a Papist
Feb.	1	John Feltham (35)
Feb.	3	Elizabeth Odbar (18), a Papist
Feb.	8	Mary Hiscock (53)
Feb.	17	Catherine Evil, an Infant
Feb.	26	Teresa Green (19), a Papist
Mar.	10	William Bond (22), from Frome
Mar.	31	Elizabeth d. of John & Elizabeth Markey†
April	2	Elizabeth Bond (56)
April	13	Mary Feltham, an Infant
April	26	Jane Owen (45)
May	10	William Edwards (73)

* There is another entry dated Nov. 11, but it is struck out and is illegible.
† This entry is struck out.

May	11	Thomas Cains (8), a Papist
May	12	Margaret Edwards (36)
May	16	Ann Edwards (50)
May	17	James Green (18)
May	25	William Green (54)
May	28	Hannah Rial (19)
May	29	John Bishop (60)
May	30	Margaret Green (48)
July	30	Margaret Baker, from y' workhouse (80)
Aug.	13	Thomas Draper, an Infant
Sep.	10	Henry Shepherd, an Infant, Papist
Sep.	11	Robert Jupe (30)
Sep.	20	Elisabeth Hurle, an Infant
Oct.	8	Ann Barker (80)
Oct.	28	Mary White (81), a Papist
Nov.	5	George Phillips (106)
Nov.	25	Owen Hill (16), found dead in a field
Dec.	14	Jane Edwards (76), from Stoke

1781.

Jan.	11	John Topp (81)
Feb.	8	Francis Feltham (75), a Papist
Mar.	23	James Baker (43)
April	7	Elizabeth Markey (75)
May	20	James Bull (82), from y' workhouse
June	9	Charles Shepherd, an Infant
July	20	Mary Winsor, an Infant
Sep.	29	M's Grace Hill (68)
Nov.	14	Ann Bracher (84)
Nov.	18	Betty Lapham & James Clements, Infants
Dec.	14	Jane Hill (62)
Dec.	19	James Baker (80)

1782.

Feb.	21	Catherine Shepherd (88), a Papist
Mar.	10	Susanna Hill (44)
Mar.	25	Benjamin Bishop (24), frozen to death on y' road under a waggon
May	12	Mary Maidment, an Infant
June	9	Mary Baker, an Infant
June	16	Jane Jupe (68)
June	25	John Rial (24)
July	5	Elisabeth Lawes (56)
July	6	M' Henry White, a Papist (77)
July	23	Elizabeth Burree (80)
Aug.	5	Joan Topp (82)
Aug.	9	Mary Walter (66)
Aug.	26	Mary Bracher (36)
Oct.	20	Mary Combes (56)
Nov.	1	James Child (60)

1783.

Feb. 16	William Jupe (23)	
Feb. 21	Hannah Lapham, an Infant	
Mar. 20	Elizabeth Edwards (26)	
June 3	Revd John Panting (51), a Romish Priest	
June 5	John Bracher (82)	
Aug. 10	Mary Topp (45)	
Sep. 3	Elizabeth Bradden (71)	
Sep. 7	Hannah Vallis (91) *	
Oct. 17	Francis Kaines, an Infant, Papist	
Nov. 14	Sarah Gant, an Infant	

1784.

Feb. 9	Rachel Turner (72)
Feb. 18	Ann Hodder, a Papist (95)
Feb. 24	Mary Odber, a Papist (72)
Mar. 14	Frances Feltham, an Infant, from ye workhouse; no tax
April 5	Margaret Trimby (12), a Pauper; no tax
April 9	Ann Lapham (58)
May 3	Ann Lush (6)
May 6	Edwd Kaines, a Papist (38), pauper
May 20	Elizabeth Miles (22), pauper
May 21	Emanuel Trimby (5), pauper
May 26	William Bracher (81)
June 5	Martha Lapham (34)
July 1	Joseph Holly (78), pauper
July 25	Mary Green (68), died 20th, Small Pox, pauper
July 25	Robert Green (67), died 22nd, Small Pox, pauper
Aug. 4	Henry Edwards (63)
Aug. 17	Mary Baker (80)
Aug. 22	Elizabeth Davis (62), a Papist
Sep. 12	Bartholomew Edwards (18)
Nov. 28	James Curtis (16), pauper
Dec. 5	Ann Cooke (100)
Dec. 26	William Andrews (57)
Dec. 28	Sarah Edwards, an Infant

1785.

Jan. 17	Eleanor Bracher (74), pauper
Feb. 15	William Edwards (85)
Mar. 27	James Meaden (76)
April 4	Francis Shepherd† (66)
April 30	Mary Hill (70)
June 12	John Lapham (72), pauper
June 12	Harriot Trimby, an Infant
July 13	John Hurle (71)
July 28	Ann Davis (32)

* "The tax for registering Burials commences Oct. 2, 1783."

† The Bonham Register describes him "of Bonham."

1786.

Aug. 1	John Clements, an Infant, drown'd at ye workhouse, pauper	
Aug. 7	Sarah Jupe (31)	
Aug. 18	Edward Edwards (35)	
Aug. 31	The Honble Hester Hoare (23), died Aug. 22^d	
Sep. 13	Sarah Jupe, an Infant, pauper	
Sep. 13	Hannah Lapham, an Infant	
Sep. 17	Henry Hoare, Esqr (80), died ye 8th	
Sep. 30	Richard Hoare, an Infant	
Nov. 9	Mary Ryal (56), pauper	
Nov. 9	Timon Ryal, an Infant, pauper	
Dec. 18	Stephen Bradden (73), pauper	

1786.

Jan. 10	Sarah Clement, an Infant, pauper
Jan. 23	Thomas Miles (13), pauper
Mar. 5	Martha Read (57)
April 27	Ann* Clement (25), from Boreton
May 3	William Read (58)
May 25	John Bradden (74)
June 20	Ann Shepherd† (64), a Papist
July 10	Mary Norris (34)
Aug. 31	Ann Jupe (42), pauper
Aug. 31	James Odbar, an Infant,‡ Papist, pauper
Sep. 8	Charles Gover (74), pauper
Sep. 24	Joseph Wyat (17), kill'd by a waggon, pauper
Oct. 8	Martha Hill (57)
Oct. 19	Honoria Edwards (74), pauper
Oct. 20	John Child (Infant)
Nov. 5	Betty Winsor (56)
Nov. 8	George Jupe§ (15), pauper
Nov. 12	Philip Markey, an Infant, pauper
Nov. 27	Sarah Oly (29)
Dec. 7	Edward Parsons (72)

1787.

Jan. 6	Francis Jupe (29)
Mar. 6	Matthew Davis (95), a Papist‖
Mar. 19	John Tabor, an Infant, 2 y^rs
Mar. 26	John Target (23)
June 20	Betty Target (25)
July 18	Martha Knight (60), pauper

* *Elizabeth* struck out.

† Bonham R. adds " relict of Francis S., of Top Lane."

‡ Bonham R. adds " s. of Joseph & Mary Odbar, of Gasper."

§ Bonham R. adds "s. of Sarah Jupe, widow, Black Shoe."

‖ Bonham R. adds " of Tucking Mill."

Aug. 27 Mr John Faugoin, from Andover (39)
Aug. 31 William s. of Charles & Elizabeth Shepperd, a Papist, 2 days old

1788.

Jan. 13 James Read, from South Brewham (23)
Jan. 30 Jane Meaden (77), pauper
Feb. 17 Sarah Lamb (79), from Bourton
Mar. 6 Catherine Barnes* (31), from Poole, a Papist
Mar. 13 Elizabeth Card, an Infant
Mar. 22 Joseph Turner (78)
Mar. 30 William Collins, an Infant
April 6 Charles Matthews, *alias* Sheppard (6), pauper
April 9 Grace Markey (64), pauper
May 29 Mr Francis Faugoin (73)
June 26 Martha Bradden, an Infant, pauper
July 8 Ann Green (6)
July 23 Joan Atkins (56), pauper
Aug. 2 Martha Edwards (70), from Top Lane, pauper
Aug. 4 Henry Davis† (9), a Papist
Sep. 24 William Ryal (22), pauper
Oct. 7 Mr Francis Bredall (70), a Papist‡
Nov. 9 Mary Philips (31), Consumption
Dec. 21 Elizabeth Owen (74), pauper

1789.

Jan. 9 Samuel Rolles (36), Small Pox
Jan. 13 Sarah Child (10), Small Pox
Feb. 1 Elizabeth Miles (67)
Mar. 7 Mary Lapham (29), Consumption
Mar. 8 Richard Lapham, an Infant, Smallpox
Mar. 17 Thomas Jupe (9), Smallpox, pauper
April 24 Stephen Bradden, an Infant, Smallpox
May 1 George Matthews (60), Epilepsy, pauper
May 14 Mary Pike§ (57)
July 3 Honor Lapham (63), Dropsy, pauper
July 3 Jane Child (19), Consumption

* Bonham R. adds "w. of John Barnes."
† Bonham R. adds "s. of Charles & Mary D., of Gasper."
‡ Bonham R. adds "of London."
§ Bonham R. "Miss Mary Pike."

July 11 Elizabeth Child (3), scalded to death by accd¹
Aug. 2 Elizabeth Laurence (60), pauper
Sep. 28 Susannah Bradden, an Infant 1 day old
Oct. 8 Thomas Santal (65)
Oct. 30 Ann Shepherd* (69)
Dec. 20 John Wyat (49), from Gillingham
Dec. 27 James Tabor (7)

1790.

Feb. 21 James Shepherd† (42), a Papist
April 19 Ann Child
April 27 The Revd Montagu Barton
April 29 Susanna Swain (74)
Sep. 3 Mary White (55)
Sep. 16 Elizabeth Arnold (27)
Oct. 12 John Owen (76), porpr
? ? Mary Andrews (78), porpr
Nov. 17 Thomas Rowe, an Infant
Dec. 7 Sarah Target (70)

1791.

Mar. 27 Susana Philips (74), porper
April 6 John Evil (78), porper
May 9 Charlotte w. of Henry Upward (24)
May 12 Martha Cruth, an Infant
May 31 Ann w. of John Odber‡ (36)
June 30 Charlotte d. of Henry Upward, infant
Aug. 28 Joseph s. of Robert & Martha Bird§ (2)
Sep. 14 James Whitaker (60), porper
Oct. 9 David Boyte (56)
Dec. 28 Lucy an infant of Jhon & Mary Philips
Dec. 31 John Davis‖ (68)

1792.

April 13 Martha d. (infant) of James & Grace Child
May 10 William Hill
June 16 James illegitimate s. of Martha Odber, late Davis¶
Aug. 9 Sarah Edwards, from Bourton (39)
Aug. 9 John Elms (21)
Sep. 13 Harriet Baker (12)
Sep. 17 Sarah Combes, an Infant

* Bonham R. adds "w. of Martin Shepherd, of Gasper."
† Bonham R. adds "husb. of Mary S., Black Shoe."
‡ Bonham R. "of Gasper."
§ Bonham R. "of Stourton Lane."
‖ Bonham R. "of Gasper."
¶ Bonham R. "1¼ year."

Oct. 25 Elizabeth Lapham (58)
Nov. 8 Charles Feltham (76), a Papist,
         paup^r
Nov. 11 Sarah Smart (67), paup^r
Nov. 12 Mary Edwards (86)
Dec. 15 Thomas Target (71)

1793.

Jan.   6 Ann Evil (43), paup^r
Feb. 12 George Williams,* an Infant
Feb. 14 Mary Markey (70), paup^r
Feb. 19 James Green, an Infant,† Papist
Feb. 21 Hannah Target (88), pauper
Mar.   8 Martha Coombes (39)
Mar. 19 Sarah Baker (20)
April 10 Sarah Jupe (45),‡ Papist, pau-
          per
May   26 David Markey (5)
June   2 Henry Sheppard, an Infant,§
          Papist
July 16 Sarah Bracher (56)
Aug. 13 Felix Hurden (23), a Papist
Sep. 29 Abraham Smart, an Infant
Oct. 17 Ann Harcourt, an Infant
Oct. 25 George Phillips (37), died sud-
          denly
Nov. 30 Sarah-Upward Target (5)

1794.

Jan.   7 Martin Odbar, an Infant, Papist
Feb. 10 Elizabeth Bishop, an Infant
Mar. 10 Martin Shepherd‖ (74), a Papist
Mar. 18 Catherine Odbar¶ (44), a Papist,
          paup^r
Mar. 22 Susannah Parsons (73)
Mar. 27 John Davis** (11), a Papist
Mar. 30 Thomas Baker (23)
April 1 Francis Shepherd†† (3), a
          Papist
April 27 Elizabeth Bradden (4)
June 16 John Harcourt (35), accidental
          death
July 23 Elizabeth Shepherd‡‡ (16), a
          Papist
Nov.   5 Mary Top (30), pauper
Nov. 25 William Evil (65), pauper

* *Phillips* struck out.
† Bonham R. adds "s. of Catharine Green,
  aged 2 days."
‡ Bonham R. "of Black Slough."
§ Bonham R. "s. of Charles & Elizabeth S.,
  aged 10 months, Gasper."
‖ Bonham R. "of Gasper."
¶ Bonham R. "of Top Lane."
** Bonham R. "Joseph D. s. of Charles &
  Mary D., Gasper."
†† Bonham R. "s. of Francis & Frances S., of
  Gasper."
‡‡ Bonham R. "d. of Stephen & Frances S.,
  Gasper."

1795.

Feb.   7 Sarah Child, an Infant
Feb. 19 Basil Hurle (82)
April 2 John Lampard (45), from
          Warminster
April 4 Grace Child (41)
April 19 Stephen Bourton (81)
May   19 James Francis (5)
May   30 Mary Draper (34)
June 11 Mileah Feltham (70)
June 24 Ann Baker (84)
July 10 Sarah Gaunt, 1 year
Aug.   7 John [*blank*] Newton, an In-
          fant
Aug. 11 Thomas Edwards (47)
Aug. 26 Elizabeth Shepherd* (13), a
          Papist
Aug. 28 Thomas Smart, an Infant
Sep.   6 William Smart, an Infant
Sep. 17 Hannah Bourton (80)
Sep. 20 Mary Andrews (37)
Oct. 18 Susan Top (23)
Oct. 19 Thomas Spencer (91)

1796.

Jan. 10 Thomas Landyk (70), a Papist
Jan. 24 Alfred Tabor, an Infant
Mar. 15 Lydia Owen (80)
April 6 Charlotte d. of Elias & Ann
          Green (3)
April 10 Joseph Charlton,† died April 7
          (18)
April 10 Betty Hartgill (47)
July 14 Joseph s. of Henry & Elizth
          Miles (11)
July 24 James an infant s. of Susanna
          Feltham
Sep.   9 Sarah d. of John & Mary Green,
          2 years
Sep. 12 Kezia an infant of Willm &
          Kezia Collins
Sep. 12 Joseph an infant of John &
          Elizth Charlton
Sep. 23 Jane w. of John Edwards (70)
Dec.   4 Mary an infant of Absolem &
          Hannah Bracher

1797.

April 9 Jane Bracher‡ (82)
May   3 Willm Bracher§ (88)

* Bonham R. "d. of Mary Shepherd, Black
  Slough."
† Bonham R. "s. of Thos & Ann Charlton, of
  Stourton."
‡ Bonham R. "wid. of John Bracher, of
  Stourton."
§ In Bonham R.

June 9 Giles s. of Robert Jupe (21)
July 16 Elenor Feltham (80)
July 27 Mary Davis* (82)
Aug. 9 Henry Miles (95)
Dec. 13 Eliz[th] an infant of J[no] & Eliz[th] Charlton
Dec. 27 Mary Bradden (88)
Dec. 31 Ann Cains† (50)

1798.

Jan. 4 Elenor Landike (87)
Mar. 16 Eliz[th] Child (79)
May 21 Mary Snook (75)
May 28 Mary Wadlow (96)
July 1 Anna infant of Tho[s] & Susanna Bracher
July 6 Ann d. of Jn[o] & Charlotte Edwards
Aug. 5 Richard Bracher (93)
Nov. 25 Valentine Philips (75)

1799.

Jan. 6 Hannah Topp (64)
Jan. 8 John Edwards (82)
Jan. 13 Will[m] Bracher (2)
Jan. 16 Will[m] an infant of Jn[o] Edwards
Jan. 20 Joseph Hilliar (41)
Mar. 4 Hannah Baker‡ (29)
Mar. 10 Sophia infant of Jane Rutley
Mar. 19 George Lapham (86)
Mar. 29 Will[m] Smart (70)
May 5 Mary Wadlow (78)
May 7 Nicholas Wadlow (76)
May 12 Henry infant of Jn[o] Marshall

* Bonham R. "Mary Elmes *alias* Davis."
† Bonham R. "widow of Edward Kaines."
‡ Bonham R. "d. of the late — Baker & Mary."

June 2 James Winsor (80)
June 9 Elias s. of Jn[o] & Mary Green
June 18 Phaniah w. of Meshach Hazard (32)
July 14 Will[m] an infant of Abraham & Sarah Smart
Oct. 22 Rodah Gover (23)
Oct. 22 Biatas Gover (19)
Nov. 12 Eliz[th] Charlton (36)
Dec. 1 Mary Hurding (85)
Dec. 16 Morice Walter (81)

1800.

Feb. 11 John Target (85)
Feb. 20 Will[m] Norris (23)
Feb. 20 Frederick s. of Alexis Green (14)
Feb. 23 Robert Davis* (89)
Feb. 27 Edward Hiscock (72)
Mar. 16 Charles an infant of Robert & Mary Bird
Mar. 18 Thomas Pearce (29)
April 6 George Edwards (24)
April 8 James s. of Robert & Martha Bird (5)
April 27 Stephen Hurding (43)
July 27 Ann d. of Tho[s] & Ann Charlton (27)
Aug. 3 Grace Bradden (46)
Aug. 31 Robert s. of Philip & Ann Miles (35)
Oct. 15 Robert s. of John & Eliz[th] Charlton (8)
Oct. 28 Ann w. of Will[m] Target (70)
Dec. 14 Mary Gover (Bruton) (89)
Dec. 18 James Curtis (79)

* In Bonham R.

INDEX.

THE END.

London: Mitchell and Hughes, Printers, 140 Wardour Street, W.

www.ingramcontent.com/pod-product-compliance
Lightning Source LLC
Chambersburg PA
CBHW031442280326
41927CB00038B/1571